"Wisdom That Transforms. Action That Lasts."

Our Commitment

We believe that true wisdom has the power to transform lives. Our mission is to equip readers with timeless insights and practical tools that inspire growth, guide decisions, and empower purposeful living. We don't just inform—we empower.

Our books combine profound understanding with real-life application, enabling readers to unlock their potential and navigate life's challenges with clarity and confidence. With each step guided by wisdom, we help you create lasting change and live the life you deserve.

When wisdom meets purpose, transformation follows.

INTEGRITY LIFE PRINCIPLE: Be honest, live with integrity, and base your life on truth.

Copyright

Choose Integrity: Honesty is the foundation for personal development, by J. S. Wellman, published by Extra-mile Publishing, Box 465, Thompsons Station, TN 37179, copyright © 2022, J. S. Wellman

ISBN   978-1-952359-30-9   (paperback)
ISBN   978-1-952359-35-4   (ebook)

This book is available as an audiobook on our Amazon Life Planning book series page:

"Practical Wisdom for Real-Life Challenges!"

For More Information About the Life Planning Series:

www.lifeplanningtools.com

Life Planning Series
by J. S. Wellman

Choose Integrity

Honesty is the foundation
for personal development.

J. S. Wellman

LIFE PLANNING SERIES
J.S. WELLMAN

Extra-mile Publishing

This book is available as an audiobook on our Amazon Life Planning book series page:

Table of Contents

Message From the Author

Unlock Your Potential with Timeless Wisdom!

The general purpose of this book and the Life Planning Series is to encourage you to pursue actions and character traits that will produce your best life. The Series addresses ten different activities or traits that help people improve their lives, and *CHOOSE Core Values* addresses sixteen separate core values that you might consider beneficial.

Understand that you can improve or acquire high personal character and outstanding habits, no matter how good or bad your life may be at the moment. Good personal character and life habits <u>can be</u> achieved.

You don't have to read all the books in this series to make a significant change or improvement in your life. Find the books that focus on the areas of your life that you want to improve and dig in.

Know that this is a progressive journey. You don't need to climb the highest mountain immediately. You may just want to learn more about the basic principles and concepts. This Series and this book will provide you with a foundation for decisions relative to your lifestyle, goals, priorities, and commitments.

The key to developing high character and making good decisions in your life is *intentionality*. The Life Planning Series will help you identify the path you want to travel but you will need to be intentional about walking that path. If you want to make progress toward the goal of living a better life, you must intentionally take action.

Change will require making good decisions, establishing important core values in your life, setting priorities, and making commitments. This book will help you identify the values in life that will produce your goals and objectives. High personal character and good habits can be achieved if you want them.

This Series is designed to help you smooth out the path for your life journey. But, remember, all actions (both words and deeds) have consequences. These consequences will impact you and all those around you.

The key to your success is: "*Decide you want to do it and work at it regularly.*"

Steve

"Set your mind on your future and commit to being the very best you can be!"
Stephen H Berkey[2]

"Wisdom to decide and the steps to succeed."

Free PDF
Living Wisely

The Life Planning Guide

A Quick-Start Guide to Purposeful Living and Wise Decisions!

Discover the five life domains: purpose, people, principles, productivity, and perspective. Wisdom is the ability to apply truth and logic to real-life decisions and produce good outcomes. It influences your choices and will produce action that lasts. Consider and apply the five practical wisdom principles for daily living. (6 pages)

Free PDF: https://getwisdompublishing.com/resource-registration/

Living Wisely
The Life Planning Guide

Wisdom That Transforms.
Action That Lasts.

Stephen H Berkey
J.S. Wellman

Free PDF

Five Practical Principles For Life

When wisdom meets purpose, transformation follows.

Free PDF
Wise Decision-Making

[Get the ebook version for 99 cents]

You can make good choices.

This free resource provides a project-oriented perspective and gives ten detailed steps to analyze issues/problems to determine a solution. (26 pages)

Good decisions expand your horizons. Don't allow the fear of decision-making paralyze your ability to make good choices. Think through the reasonable alternatives and move forward. When your eyes are on the goal, making good decisions is easier.

Free PDF: https://getwisdompublishing.com/resource-registration/

Kindle ebook for 99 cents: https://www.amazon.com/dp/B09SYGWRVL/

Ebook

Free PDF

Make Thoughtful Decisions!

Good decisions expand your horizons.

The Life Planning Series provides real-life tools for wise decision-making and personal transformation

Wisdom to Decide.
Steps to Succeed.
Life Starts Here!

Chapter 1 – Introduction

Life Planning Based on Wisdom!
Build Wisdom. Build Life!

We want to inform, encourage, and inspire you to choose character and improve your life.

The second and equally important purpose is to help you implement specific changes in your life.

Our third goal is to encourage you to pass it on. It is our desire that you will not only obtain this knowledge, but pass it on to others – particularly friends, children, grandchildren, or students.

An African proverb says, *"Don't spend all day rejoicing on your bench. When you pray, move your feet!"* The message of this proverb is that if you want to accomplish something, nothing will happen if you're sitting on your bench all day.

Growth and improvement, including living a better life, requires action and intentionality. The good news is that you can use the information in this book to acquire knowledge that will help you follow a path to a better life.

Those who want to develop a _total life plan_ can do that by acquiring our *Life Planning Handbook*. We will discuss that book later in this chapter.

WHY READ THIS BOOK

The ideal reader of this book is someone who wants to accomplish any of the following:

- learn more about this subject,
- improve your life circumstances,
- live a better life with less stress,
- dig more deeply into the meaning of this subject and how it might impact your life,
- overcome the chaos of life, family or work relationships, or
- learn how to make good or better decisions.

PERSONAL GROWTH

We encourage you to make good choices and improve your personal and family life. This process is often referred to as personal growth or personal development. There are many good reasons for pursuing personal growth in your life:

- to find personal peace, meaning, and purpose,
- to gain more control over life situations,
- to acquire certain skills or abilities,
- to become more disciplined,
- to improve or overcome negative attitudes,
- to expand your horizons,
- to make better decisions,
- to open new avenues of understanding, or
- to change certain outcomes in your life.

It is our hope that this book will help you identify conditions in your life you would like to improve. You may need only some help focusing on the right things. You may just want guidance in finding things you can tweak to make a few changes in your lifestyle. You may want a clearer vision of your goals. Or you may want to do some serious work on some particular aspect of your life. Our Life Planning Series will help you achieve any of these goals and desires.

ABOUT *CHOOSE Integrity*

Build a life you're proud of—one decision at a time.

What if your word carried undeniable weight—and your character inspired trust, admiration, and success?
In a world full of shortcuts, spin, and self-interest, living with integrity isn't just admirable—it's transformative. Integrity shapes how you think, act, lead, and love. It defines who you are.

Choose Integrity is your guide to becoming the kind of person others trust and deeply respect. Whether you're starting fresh or strengthening the values you already hold, this powerful, practical book will walk you step-by-step toward a life grounded in truth, honesty, and purpose.

In these pages you'll discover how to:

- Cultivate integrity as a core value—not just a good idea
- Strengthen your personal character through small, consistent choices
- Align your lifestyle, goals, and priorities with your beliefs

- Make decisions that reflect your highest self—even under pressure
- Earn the kind of trust that opens doors and deepens relationships

This isn't about perfection—it's about progress. You'll learn how to build a rock-solid foundation for life planning and character development, regardless of where you're starting. With clear strategies and encouragement, you'll begin to take control of your future—one intentional decision at a time.

If you've ever wanted to feel proud of who you are, how you live, and the impact you make—this book is for you.

Become someone the world can count on.

THE LIFE PLANNING SERIES

The Life Planning Series covers most of the important subjects that you would address in an attempt to live a good or better life. Most of the books address one particular subject, help you identify your life goals, and guide you in creating action plans to achieve those goals. One exception is the Life Planning Handbook which will help you develop a complete life plan.

The Series in total addresses such topics as integrity, choosing friends, guarding your speech, working with diligence, making sound financial decisions, having a positive self- image, leadership, faith, choosing core values, and love and family.

Core values of The Life Planning Series

The Life Planning books are developed around ten core values and principles:

1. Wise sayings, parables, proverbs, common sense, and street smarts provide an underlying foundation for gaining knowledge, understanding, and wisdom.

2. Honesty, integrity, and living a life based on truth are the foundational character traits for achieving a life of hope and contentment. They are the cornerstones to living a better life.

3. There are five Primary Life Principles:

    - be honest, live with integrity, and base your life on truth,
    - choose your friends wisely,
    - choose your words carefully,
    - be a diligent and hard worker, and
    - make sound financial choices.

4. Life change is possible. You can make positive changes and expect good results to follow, but all choices have consequences.

5. It is not necessary to change a large number of character traits in order to achieve significant life improvement. Changing a few *key* areas can have a major impact on your quality of life.

6. The key to making any life change is *intentionality*.

7. Perfection is not possible, but if you aim for it, you can achieve significant results. Nothing will be attained if you do not try.

8. We will be open about the difficulties, barriers, and walls that you might experience in implementing life change. Understand that barriers can be torn down.

9. The ultimate purpose in this series is to develop an effective plan for improving life circumstances. It is not our intent to provide lengthy textbooks on the particular subjects. Our presentation of the text material will be limited to what you need to know in order to develop an effective plan to improve your life.

10. Life is a progressive journey requiring good choices and a solid foundation for the future. Time is needed to implement change. Patience and perseverance will be necessary to achieve the desired results.

Transform Your thinking.
Transform Your Life!

THE BOOKS

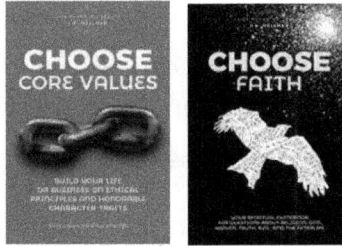

Go to the Life Planning Series page
to choose the book you want:

https://www.amazon.com/dp/B09TH9SYC4

THE LIFE PLANNING HANDBOOK

This is a unique book in the Life Planning Series. The purpose is to produce a total and complete *Life Plan* for your life. The sections include:

1. Life Principles and Character Attributes
2. Habits
3. Friends and Family Relationships
4. Work and Work Ethic
5. Education
6. Community Service
7. Money and Wealth
8. Health
9. Spiritual

The planning process in the Handbook will examine your skills and abilities, your personal life values, priorities, and commitments. The book will help you identify your life goals and create action steps to achieve those goals.

This book will generate purpose, direction, and growth in your life.

Go to https://www.amazon.com/dp/1952359325
to get your copy now.

Decision Fatigue Ends Here!
A structured approach to turn wisdom into results.

Chapter 2
Consequences

"Mess with the bull and
one usually gets the horns."
Latin American saying[3]

GENERAL

Consequences are a vital concept in our understanding of making good choices and setting goals to have a successful life. Thus, this chapter on consequences will appear in most of the books in the Life Planning Series.

You have complete freedom to choose what you want to do, but you cannot choose the consequences. Thus, poor choices can be a disaster. We bear the consequences of our words and actions. It is like a law of nature.

Imagine a person who consistently tells small lies at work to cover for missed deadlines or incomplete tasks. At first, the consequences seem minor, but over time, the lies pile up. Eventually the deception is discovered and trust is broken. The company loses business, the employee is terminated, and their professional reputation is severely damaged. This downward spiral began with a simple refusal to be honest.

If you don't want to suffer the negative results of poor decisions, think in advance what your actions are likely to produce. What you do and what you say will have lasting impact on yourself and on others.

THERE WILL BE CONSEQUENCES

Life is a series of decisions and choices. We are constantly making choices about both significant and insignificant things. Choices shape the course of our lives. Some people learn a great deal from the consequences of their actions and others seem oblivious.

Consider someone who falsifies parts of their résumé to land a job. At first, the lie seems harmless because they got the position. But when real responsibilities arise that require the claimed experience their inability to perform becomes obvious. The result can be embarrassment, job loss, and even a damaged reputation that can follow them for years.

Physical consequences are a law of nature. If you touch a hot stove you will get burned. If you walk into the street in front of a truck you will be injured. Behaviors have predictable consequences as well. If you cheat and lie, people will stop doing business with you and your reputation will suffer. If you are not dependable, people will no longer trust you.

By definition consequences occur as a result of something else happening. The result may occur immediately or it could take a while, even years. This is often one of the reasons that we make poor choices – the consequence does not occur immediately and because of this we think there will never be consequences.

The actual consequences you experience will vary depending on your circumstances, but there will be consequences nonetheless. The degree or size of the consequence will also vary, but we should not be fooled into thinking small transgressions have no consequences.

*"One who steals has no right
to complain if he is robbed."*
Aesop[4]

THE FARMER AND THE OX

There was a farmer who had been plowing hard for many days with an ox and mule yoked together. The ox told the mule that they should pretend to be sick and rest. The mule declined saying, "No, we must get the work done, for the season is short." But the ox played sick and the farmer brought him hay and corn and made him comfortable.

When the mule came in from plowing the ox asked how things had gone. The mule said, "We didn't get as much done but we did okay, I guess." The ox asked, "Did the old man say anything about me?" Nothing," said the mule. The next day the ox played sick again. When the tired mule came in he asked again how it went. "All right, but we sure didn't get much done." The ox asked, "What did the old man say about me?" The mule replied, "Nothing directly to me, but he had a long talk with the butcher."[5]

This is similar to the message in the story concerning the consequences of a hearty breakfast to the chicken and the pig. A breakfast of ham and eggs to the chicken is a temporary inconvenience, but to the pig it is a permanent and lasting consequence – breakfast is a <u>real</u> commitment.

All actions have consequences!

COUNT THE COST

Someone has said that you will ultimately be invited to a party where you will dine on your own consequences. Whether your actions were wise or unwise, you will eventually bear the consequences. Thus, it is important to think about the consequences in advance. What will result from your words or actions?

Regardless of the particular situation, it will always be easier to arrive at a positive outcome if you have thought ahead, evaluated the circumstances, and determined in advance how you will respond to the important challenges that arise in your life.

Consider the teenager who lies to their parents about where they're going and who they're with. When something goes wrong, like an accident or an encounter with law enforcement, the trust between child and parent is shattered. Rebuilding that trust can take years, and depending on the circumstances, may never fully be restored.

What you do and say in questionable circumstances will have a lasting impact on your life. Emblazon the following truth in your mind and on your heart:

> *Consequences shape lives.*
> *Choices produce consequences*
> *which direct the course of life.*
> *Therefore, count the cost!*

LEGACY

Our words and actions can have an impact for a long time. The ongoing impact of poor behavior is a concept that escapes many people. Poor decisions can affect a family for many generations. Bad behavior establishes a pattern that becomes the blueprint for a child's future behavior.

The experiences children have or observe become their normal responses in similar situations. What is witnessed by small children is later reproduced. They can learn to be trustworthy, reliable, and dependable, or they can learn to do drugs, smoke, and gossip. What a child sees modeled in the home becomes the normal response, and that behavior cycle can continue into many future generations.

Your legacy extends into future generations; therefore, be sure that it is a positive one! Most people have no concept of how their behavior can impact the future. This is dramatically demonstrated by comparing the lives of Jonathan Edwards and Max Jukes.

Jonathan Edwards was a Puritan preacher in the 1700s. His descendants demonstrate the powerful influence of wise choices and a godly life. At the turn of the 20th century, A. E. Winship decided to trace the descendants of Jonathan Edwards and compare them to a man known as Max Jukes.

Mr. Jukes was incarcerated in the New York prison system at the time Jonathan Edwards was preaching. Winship found that 42 of the men in the New York prison system could trace their heritage back to Max Jukes. Jukes, an atheist, lived a godless life. He married an ungodly woman, and from the descendants of this union 310 died as paupers, 150 were criminals, 7 were murderers, and more than half of the women were prostitutes.

In contrast, the record of Jonathan Edwards' progeny tells a much different story. An investigation of 1,394 known descendants of Jonathan Edwards revealed

- 13 college presidents,
- 65 college professors,
- 3 United States Senators,
- 30 judges,
- 100 lawyers,
- 60 physicians,
- 75 army and navy officers,
- 100 preachers and missionaries,
- 60 authors of prominence,
- 1 Vice-President of the United States,
- 80 public officials in other capacities,
- 295 college graduates.

Today, instead of the blessings like those that came to Jonathan Edwards' progeny, we are seeing a growing multitude like the descendants of Max Jukes! Have you seen a family in which the grandfather was an alcoholic – and his sons and grandsons abuse alcohol, too? Have you seen a family plagued with sickness, drug abuse, debt, or poverty? Often that is because someone in the past did not make good choices. We are going to leave a legacy for our children and grandchildren. Will we pass on a blessing or a curse?[8]

> *Your actions, both good and bad, establish the foundation of your life, lifestyle, and legacy.*

We reap what we sow

In a number of his proverbs, King Solomon suggests that doing what is right is to be preferred over evil. King

Solomon was known world-wide for his great wisdom. He wrote and recorded many proverbs recognized for their practical insight and wisdom. He describes the nature of righteousness as being immovable and that it will stand above evil.

Is your desire for doing what is "right" rooted deeply or is it planted in shallow soil that can easily be washed away? Solomon indicated that the wicked would ultimately be overthrown and that the righteous would survive because their character had roots that were deep and impossible to dislodge.

Solomon argued that it is better to be on the side of the righteous. The reasoning is the same as the man who chooses to build his house, business, or life on rock versus sand. If we build on sand (questionable ways) then our hopes and plans will never stand up against the storms of life. If we build on rock (high character) our plans should hold firm.

We do reap what we sow and if we sow badly because we have rejected what is right, the wise counsel of friends, or ethical core values, we will reap the negative consequences. Those who think they know everything frequently reject wisdom and follow their own plans and schemes. It has been said that those who insist on following their poorly chosen ways will often end up choking on them.

Lysa Terkeurst in her book, *The Best Yes,* says this about making decisions: "The decision you make determines the schedule you keep. The schedule you keep determines the life you live. And how you live your life determines how you spend your soul."

Think about that statement. You could say this truth in a number of ways – Ms. Terkeurst chose this particular description. But any way you say it the meaning is, *your decisions determine your life*. The consequences of your decisions constitute your day and your future. You are always living in the midst of the choices you make; therefore, make good choices. The consequences will determine how you live your life, or in Terkeurst's words, how you "spend your soul."

For example, consider a person who lives with unwavering integrity. They are known for telling the truth, even when it's uncomfortable or risky. Because of this, others trust them deeply and seek their input on important matters. When a promotion opportunity arises, this individual is likely the clear choice—not just for their competence, but for their character. Integrity doesn't just prevent negative consequences it also opens doors to greater opportunities and success.

IT'S NOT FAIR

Unfortunately, life is not fair. Worrying about fairness, arguing about it, or fighting it will be of little value. Being "fair" generally means that everyone is treated equally (the concept of socialism). But life is not fair!
If you believe that life is intended to be fair, then it's not fair to others less fortunate that you were born in America and are therefore privileged. It is not fair that you have avoided poverty, wars, terrorism, natural disasters, tyrants, dying in an accident, abuse . . .

Obviously it is unrealistic to argue it's not fair that we experience the consequences of our own poor choices, especially since we are the ones making those poor choices. If we think we shouldn't incur the result of our poor choices then we certainly should not expect to experience the rewards of our good choices.

For example a small business owner faced a dilemma: report an error that will cost the company money or hide it and hope the employees don't find out. Choosing honesty, they disclose the mistake. Though there is short-term financial loss and some business disruption, the long-term gain is immense: the employees respect the leader more, clients appreciate the transparency, and trust in the company grows. The consequence of honesty is not always immediate reward, but may assure long-term stability and a solid reputation.

Think about the consequences,
then choose wisely!

WHO TO BLAME

Blame is a big concern for many people today. When something bad happens, the first reaction by many is to find someone to blame. Many people no longer accept the concept of an "accident." It's become the cultural norm to assign blame and "make someone pay."

Some of us react in illogical ways to consequences. The most illogical is the person who totally ignores the obvious dangers of what they are about to do and then rather than accepting the consequences, casts blame. They become angry or embarrassed and attempt to find someone or something to blame in order to take the attention off their own poor judgment.

Taking responsibility for mistakes, misunderstandings, or accidents is becoming a lost art. Many children have been raised to believe they do not have to suffer consequences.

MISTAKES!

What happens when we make a mistake? A mistake is not the end of the world – it's a mistake, not a death sentence! If we make a wrong choice, we must rethink the issue and select another path. We all make mistakes. The real challenge in life is how we handle those mistakes.

Think about a married couple where one partner has been hiding a financial debt. When the debt is discovered, the shock creates emotional turmoil, mistrust, and relational strain. While the situation could have been handled constructively early on, the prolonged deception intensified the damage. Being honest from the beginning, even when it's uncomfortable, is always the better path.

Not every choice we make will be the right decision. Expect some failures in life and don't be overwhelmed if what you choose does not work out as you expect. If the choice was bad, wrong, or ill-advised, fix it!

> *Admitting mistakes and taking responsibility*
> *is a characteristic of those who*
> *are living their best life.*

BARRIERS

Difficulties and barriers can be overcome if you are determined to find a solution. It's a lot easier to make changes in life if you are receiving guidance and help. In addition to our books we suggest finding someone to join you in improving your life circumstances. If you cannot find someone to participate with you, find someone you can meet with weekly or periodically to discuss your progress, your difficulties, your needs, and most of all, your successes.

Here are some effective ways to overcome personal barriers:

1. Recognize that many barriers are in reality just excuses.
2. Recruit a support person (friend) to hold you accountable.
3. Recruit others to do it with you.
4. Recruit support from your family.
5. If time is a hurdle – work it out. Adjust your schedule and priorities.

Do not expect change, improvement, or miracles overnight. Ask for help when you need it.

> *"Being challenged in life is inevitable,*
> *being defeated is optional."*
> Roger Crawford[9]

TIPS TO AVOID UNINTENDED CONSEQUENCES

Here are five tips you could adopt before making decisions:

1. **THINK** before you act.
    Take time to consider the consequences.
    Ask yourself, "What would 'wisdom' do?"
    Think logically.

2. **LISTEN** to the advice of others.
    Seek out trusted friends.

3. <u>CONSIDER</u> the pros and cons.
How will this decision impact me or others?
Will I be proud of the outcome?
What would my friends think?

4. <u>BE PATIENT</u>.
"Sleep on it" is often excellent advice.
Research as much as you can.

5. <u>EMOTIONS</u> often cause poor decisions.
Base your choices on facts and reality, not feelings.
Do not make decisions based on your emotions.

TIPS YOU COULD USE

a. Underline, circle, or highlight the tips above or anything in this chapter that you think could make the most impact if you implemented them in your life. You will revisit these choices at the end of the book in the Planning section.

b. There may be other things that you think would make a difference. Write them below:

_____
_____
_____
_____

"It is the peculiar quality of a fool to perceive
the faults of others and to forget his own."
Cicero[10]

Chapter 3

INTEGRITY LIFE PRINCIPLE

Your character and your life begin with a blank slate.
Life is what you make it.

Our personal character is the foundation of who we are. It determines what we say and what we do as well as the habits we form. Our character reflects what we really believe and what we value. If we have the inherent desire to do what is right we will likely have a high regard for truth and integrity. If our sense of right and wrong is blurred, then our adherence to attributes that produce high character may also be blurred.

This book in our Life Planning Series focuses on honesty, integrity, and truth, which we believe are the fundamental attributes that influence or determine our personal character and our ability to live a successful life. The Series will include separate books on reputation, leadership, identity and wisdom under the category of "Personal Character."

A person of high character does the right thing whether or not someone is watching. Others may think it is acceptable to do almost anything as long as they don't get caught. History and experience demonstrate that questionable behavior is almost always found out and the people involved suffer for such behavior. Reputations can be damaged beyond repair by poor personal character traits.

Someone who is honest and truthful will be respected and be known for their high character. Jimi Hendrix has said, "The best index to a person's character is how he treats people who can't do him any good, and how he treats people who can't fight back."[11] The point that Hendrix is making is that the situation or circumstances do not necessarily matter. Someone of high character will do what is right.

We believe that high character is the fundamental characteristic of one who desires to live a successful life, and honesty, integrity, and truth are the foundational traits underlying that life. Thus, these traits are the foundation of the five Primary Life Principles, the first of which is the:

INTEGRITY LIFE PRINCIPLE:

Be honest, live with integrity, and base your life on truth.

It is our belief that of the five Primary Life Principles, being a person of integrity is of primary importance. If you adopt or claim this principle for your life, you will make great strides toward living a better life. Honesty, integrity, and truth are the gateways to being the best you. You will never be able to be all you can be if these traits are not fundamental attributes in your life.

Any contractor or builder will tell you that the most important part of a house is the foundation. If the foundation is not level and setting on solid ground (or rock if you live in Tennessee) it will create problems in every phase of the building process. The workers will continually be making adjustments and alterations to account for the problem. It's so easy to forget to make the necessary adjustments in all phases of the building process and then at some point you are faced with the need to make serious and expensive changes because someone forgot to adjust for the problem. The issues can become so great that the construction needs to be torn out, or the owner will have to live with something that is unacceptable.

The Primary Life Principles are to living your best life as a foundation is to a house. Honesty, integrity, and truth are the cornerstones of those Life Principles. If one's life is not built on honesty and truth it will be very difficult to end up with a life that is in balance. Oh yes, you can get by, but the scars of a life built on something other than integrity is like the house where everything on the floor rolls toward the street because the foundation is not level. The house has not fallen down but living in it is frustrating and difficult.

If you live with integrity, you will automatically or inherently possess a number of other good character traits. Integrity will produce a life in which you are dependable, reliable, upright, a person of good reputation, etc. I might even suggest that if you live out this Life Principle you will be:

- righteous in the sight of God,
- admired in the sight of man, and
- honored by friends, family, and associates.

That is an amazingly simple concept if you think about it! Stop and consider for a moment how you could offend God or man if you are honest and base your life on truth?

Let's assume for the moment that these characteristics are absolutely true in your life. What would God or man find lacking in you? What essential character trait would you lack? If you think we are overstating the importance of these characteristics try to think of a positive character trait where that trait can exist without you being honest and true.

If you are truthful you will be sincere, incorruptible, equitable, and just. You will be guided by and make choices based on truth. You will not be dishonest, a liar, or a gossip. You will not be devious, deceptive, crafty, cagy, scheming, double-dealing, false, or deceptive. Truth will be a major component in your life.

*Make it your primary life goal to be honest,
live with integrity, and
base your life on truth!*

Wisdom to Action Challenge

Reflect on a situation where you demonstrated integrity. How did it impact your sense of self and your relationships? Identify one area in your life where you can further embody integrity and commit to taking action this week.

Chapter 4

HONESTY

"Truth is the secret of eloquence and of virtue,
the basis of moral authority; it is the
highest summit of art and of life."
Henri Frederic Amiel[12]

GENERAL

In the quote above, Amiel recognizes truth as the fundamental foundation of character and he even relates it to life itself. Honesty and truth cannot be denied as the cornerstones of character. They support and are integrated into all parts of our other character traits.

Honesty means that you speak the truth. You do not lie. It also means that you do not steal, rob, or cheat anybody. You would not defraud, deceive, ensnare, con, misguide, or misinform someone.

Truth and honesty can be illustrated by the color white. If something is true and honest, then it is pure white. If there is any gray then it is no longer white. It may be referred to as dirty white, off-white, or cream. Truth and honesty are like that. They are pure. There is no such thing as partial truth. Something is either true or is not true.

You are either honest or you're not honest. If there is any gray mixed into your truth, then it is no longer true. Little white lies should be called little gray lies. Partial truth and partial honesty do not exist.

HONESTY IN ALL THINGS

If you are honest then you will be honest in both the big and small things of life. It doesn't matter if it is stealing pencils from your employer or stealing a car. The honest person does neither. There is no such thing as a little lie, a little deception, or a little cheating. If we cheat at little things we are likely to cheat at big things.

More importantly, if you know someone who does not cheat on the little things, that person is not likely to cheat on big things. You can trust a person who demonstrates honesty, dependability, and reliability in the little things of life. An honest man is honest with pennies as well as with millions.

If you are seeking people of high character and integrity in your life or work, examine their other character traits to determine if they support integrity and truth. If a person is not genuine, authentic, and sincere, you have reason to question their integrity.

THE SURVEY SAYS

Men and women were asked what they lie about and the following is a summary of what they said according to a survey of over 1,200 Americans conducted by the financial website CreditDonkey.com.

1. 27.7% of men *lied about their accomplishments*, compared with only 16.8 percent of women.
2. 24.1% of men *lied on their Facebook profile* versus 16.6 percent of women.
3. 21.7% of men acknowledged they *lied on a resume*, compared with 16.3 percent of women.
4. 42.1% of men *haven't told the truth about their financial well-being* versus 37.6 percent of women.
5. 17.4% of men *lied to their doctors*, compared to 25.6 percent of women.

Assuming most survey respondents were honest about their bent for lying (which seems like an oxymoron), more than three-quarters of the participants in the survey believed lying was acceptable in some cases. Ninety percent of the survey participants thought everyone lied, *so at any given moment, it may be impossible to know who's telling the truth.* This is a telling reflection on our society and on the subject of truth.

When participants were asked to identify the topics they most often lied about, men revealed they prefer to bluff about money and their accomplishments while women are more likely to be less than truthful about their health and appearance. One of the few things men and women both do in equal amount is lie to those who should know them better than anyone: their friends and family. Generally, the survey indicated that men and women lie to parents and friends about 40% of the time and to siblings and significant others about 20% of the time. That is sad![13]

In another massive study involving nearly 70,000 U.S. college and high school students, 70% admitted to cheating. The Duke University report also indicated that Internet plagiarism had quadrupled in the previous six years. A separate poll of 25,000 high schoolers found that nearly half agreed with the statement, "A person has to lie or cheat sometimes in order to succeed."[14]

This problem is not limited to the young. Adults have similar attitudes. According to a Reader's Digest survey of 2,624 readers, 13% had blamed a co-worker for something they did, 18% had lied on a resume or job application, and 32% had lied to their spouse about the cost of a recent purchase. And, not surprisingly, 63% had called in sick at work when they were not sick.[15]

It would seem that we are living in an age of liars! Who, in fact, can we trust? The answer would seem to be – nobody! In days such as these it is difficult to trust anything you hear or read. Fake news seems to be all around us. In fact, it is extremely difficult to get actual news – everyone has an agenda and opinion. Propaganda, disguised as news, is being distributed daily from most news outlets.

Who do you personally trust today? Why? If you are not suspicious about what you hear or read you are in greater danger than you may realize. Today, it is often necessary to confirm statements and opinions by doing your own research.

We must be extremely cautious about who we believe and who we trust. Too many people are calling their agenda the truth because they have a position they want to promote. Others just like to hear themselves talk and take positions that put themselves in the limelight, on talk shows, or in the middle of a social media buzz.

> *"If a person doesn't lie,*
> *he won't have that much to remember!"*
> Abe Lincoln[16]

LIES, BIG and SMALL

What's the difference between stealing a $5 product from the mall or one that costs $5000? Technically nothing: both are stealing. Certainly one is a more significant loss to the owner. One is probably an impulse steal and the other a planned felony. An important question becomes, "Should the punishment be the same or different for these two offenses?" If punishment is to be for the edification or rehabilitation of the villain, then why would there be different punishments? The one who stole something small today is very likely to steal something big tomorrow. The only legal difference in the two scenarios is the value of the item taken.

If you believe it is acceptable to steal small items without incurring any punishment, then you will also find it acceptable to lie about small things. The problem occurs when someone must decide what is small and what is large. Who has such authority? How much authority do they have to define what is important and what is not? What if one small thievery combined with a hundred other small thieveries was enough to put someone out of business?

What if the little lie has far more implications that anyone could know about?

Are lies that protect people's feelings acceptable? What if the lie is simply more convenient and protects you from answering many unnecessary questions? There are all kinds of little lies that are convenient. For example, instead of telling someone you don't like their friends, you tell them you are not feeling well and cannot come to their party. Are these lies acceptable?

Many of these "little lies" are social lies that keep one from hurting another unnecessarily. If this is commonplace for you, how often do you find it necessary to tell such lies? What are your real motives? Do these lies violate your core values? It may be acceptable to tell a white lie but it should be a calculated and conscious decision.

A big danger in little lies is that they can lead to the habit of lying. Instead of just lying about trivia or matters of little consequence, we begin lying to protect ourselves from our own poor choices.

If we do not want to look bad to our friends or if we fail to complete a promise, it becomes easy to lie. Lying can become a very convenient part of our lifestyle, allowing us to make excuses for not fulfilling a promise, not being dependable, or being unreliable.

Don't lie!

SOCIETY ACCEPTANCE

Society changes when dishonesty is out of control or rampant throughout the general public. Cheating or any dishonest behavior can become a way of life and be accepted as a normal state of affairs. For example, you can't do business in some countries and even with some city or state governments without paying bribes.

Dishonesty left unchecked becomes a cancer controlling how business is conducted.

It can become so bad that dishonesty becomes the norm. When the general public decides everyone is doing it, they believe they must cheat in order to survive. This is what happened in the sport of professional bicycle racing between 1990 and 2010. You may have read about the drug scandals involving Lance Armstrong. But Armstrong was not the only one cheating. The sport was overrun by cheating and drug abuse.

Then, of course, the cover-up begins. Everyone lies about the true environment, hoping not to be caught. The sad thing is that the lying just builds up until it explodes. The liars begin thinking that what they are doing is acceptable and not dishonest. They believe their own lies. They may even have a very high opinion of themselves while they are living a lie. But eventually the lie is exposed and the inevitable cover-up begins, leading to the undeniable result that dishonesty reigns!

Lies can make life miserable!

LIARS

Liars are usually caught or found out. Fortunes can be lost and reputations destroyed. Liars can lose their families and friends. How does this happen? Tainted riches tend to vanish, disappear, or produce negative results causing other serious problems. Difficulties tend to haunt those who live off lies. Marriages are often destroyed by lies and cheating.

The overall result is that the liar ultimately gets caught and their dishonesty will cause various levels of difficulty, suffering, and even time in prison. Some have even committed suicide because they could not live with the shame of dishonesty.

So what's the answer in such a situation?

Admit the mistake. Admit when you are wrong or have done something wrong that resulted in an unintended consequence. If necessary, throw yourself on the mercy of those you have harmed. One of the most difficult things to do is to admit wrong doing. It's not easy. But, it's the only thing to do to fix the situation.

A personal admission of error or misdoing is the best solution to righting a wrong. If Lance Armstrong had admitted his cheating early on and offered to help fix the problem, his life would have been much different and his standing in the eyes of society would be much higher today.

> *"I have met men who are habitual liars.*
> *They have lied so long that they no longer*
> *can distinguish between the truth and a lie.*
> *Their sensitivity to sin has been*
> *almost completely deadened."*
> Billy Graham[17]

HONESTY MATTERS

Being honest is like eating a sweet piece of chocolate. Why? Because it is so desirable and sweet it can produce a very comfortable and satisfying feeling. Honesty should be desired like foods that give us great pleasure. Knowing you are honest and your life is based on truth will produce a life of satisfaction and far less stress than one that exists on lies.

Cheaters are deceptive or fraudulent people who attempt to fool or trick someone. Do you have any friends or associates whom you would describe like this? If you do, you are not likely very good friends because you cannot trust them. Their lives are heavy with stress, strain, and pressure because they must continually lie to support their dishonesty.

Do you know anyone you consider a liar? Are they one of your friends or associates? Do you hang out with them? Why? People who are pathological liars are very difficult to live or work with.

I knew someone for a number of years before I figured out that he was a liar. He had clients that were always mad at him and he would tell me stories about why they were crazy, misinformed, or lying. I believed him because I had no reason to think otherwise.

After a number of years I caught him lying to me – serious fabrications that in the end cost me a lot of money. This man never took responsibility for his mistakes, or failure to keep his promises. He would never admit he was wrong and he always had an excuse, usually a lie. I think he was embarrassed to admit any kind of failure, mistake, or poor decision that made him look bad, so he lied about it.

The result was that I had to stop doing business with him and drop him from my circle of friends and generally have nothing to do with him. His core values and my core values were at odds and I could not trust him. I haven't talked with him again and his current life reflects his poor choices.

But a trustworthy friend can be appreciated, trusted, and relied on for the truth. A life of honesty is one that others will see and admire. A trustworthy person is one whom you want as a friend because:

Honesty does matter!

DISHONESTY

How do you react when you catch someone lying to you? Are you are disappointed in their unreliability? Do you react in a way that would condone their lying and dishonesty? Do you respond in a way that allows them to think you have no personal standards with respect to the truth? If you act in any way that implies you understand or condone lying, you have not done yourself or the liar any favors.

The liar will probably perceive that you have little concern for truth, thus, you are not one who can be trusted. This could have significant impact on your reputation with the liar and anyone he tells about your behavior. The liar will continue to lie to you, causing you all kinds of grief.

Confronting dishonesty and unreliability can be difficult. It can be stressful. But allowing it to continue will not make a bad situation better: it will only get worse. You must make it clear to the liar that you know the truth, that you are disappointed in his behavior, and that your hope is that it never happens again.

You must communicate this gently and in a loving but forceful manner. It may even be appropriate, if the situation could recur, to outline the consequences if it happens again. The circumstances and situation should dictate how you respond.

If your one-on-one confrontation does not solve the problem, then it might be wise that you say the same thing again, but bring along a friend whom the liar respects to help emphasize the importance of being truthful. If that doesn't work, then you may have to bring the situation to the attention of someone in authority, if that is appropriate. Alternatively you may need to end the relationship.

"A liar deceives himself more than anyone,
for he believes he can remain
a person of good character when he cannot."
Richelle E. Goodrich[18]

CONSEQUENCES

The consequences of dishonesty can be many and varied.
The most frequent is that you are corrected or rebuked,
hopefully in private. But in some situations the correction
may occur in a public setting, causing shame and
embarrassment.

One of the most debilitating results of dishonesty is the
fear and worry that occurs as a result of the stress of trying
not to be caught lying. Such stress occurs because
discovery could lead to loss of friendship, respect, and
even loss of a job or family.

Another cause of anxiety is that your lies could hurt or
damage someone else. Others could be blamed for your
mistakes and they may produce ugly consequences. What
will you do if that happens? Punishment resulting from
dishonesty is often unforgiving and final.

The consequences could border on the extreme depending
on the circumstances. You might experience hate and any
resulting revenge. You could be shunned and alienated
from friends or co-workers. The situation might produce
depression, delusion, illness, and even suicide. This may
sound very dramatic if you are young or have not ever
been dishonest in a significant way. Be assured that your
heart and conscience know you are being dishonest and
they can play havoc with your well-being.

But your problems are not necessarily all centered around guilt. You may lose self-confidence, feel incompetent, or experience failures in your life, just because you made a decision to be dishonest.

TIPS FOR BEING HONEST

1. HOW TO BE HONEST

Use these tips to understand how you might respond in a given situation. Ask yourself if this is the way you normally react or do you respond differently. If so, why?

> a. Admit mistakes or errors immediately.
> b. Report incidents accurately, Don't conveniently leave out important facts.
> c. Be truthful about your involvement, even if the truth will hurt.
> d. Share true feelings and emotions honestly. Don't mask them with lies.
> e. Remove emotion from a situation. Don't respond based on emotions or feelings.
> f. Think about what you are going to say. Don't respond off the top of your head.
> g. Guard against jealousy causing you to stretch the truth.

2. REASONS YOU TEND TO LIE

There are a number of scenarios where the circumstances make it easy to lie. If you know these situations in advance you can protect yourself by being prepared.

a. Don't lie to protect or help others.

b. Don't lie to cover up something you feel guilty about.

c. Don't make promises you can't or won't keep.

d. Don't make promises that depend on someone else keeping a promise.

d. Don't exaggerate. Make sure your statements are accurate.

e. Don't be impatient. Don't respond too quickly. Think about your words.

3. CHECK YOURSELF

There are certain characteristics that often occur when one is being dishonest. It's good to be aware of these tendencies so that when they occur, you will be forewarned.

a. What is your body language? Are you nervousness, twitching, have a strained facial expression, refuse eye contact, or stand with crossed arms?

b. What are you thinking? Are you trying to think of an excuse? Are you going to be evasive, contradictory, illogical, or unreasonable in what you say?

c. Could your audience think what you are about to say is strange or outside the norm?

d. Would it be better to remain silent?

e. Would changing the subject be wise?

TIPS I COULD USE

a. Underline, circle, or highlight the 1 to 3 tips above that you think could make the most impact if you implemented them in your life. You will revisit these choices at the end of the book in the Planning section.

b. There may be other things that you think would make a difference. Write them below:

_____

_____

_____

_____

Wisdom to Action Challenge

Reflect on a time when you were dishonest. What were the consequences, and how did it affect your relationships? Identify one area where you can practice greater honesty this week, and commit to upholding the truth, even when it's difficult.

Chapter 5
INTEGRITY

"Wisdom is knowing the right path to take.
Integrity is taking it."
Immanuel Kant[19]

Integrity is the attribute of being honest, truthful, trustworthy, and compliant to a set of moral standards. Some might suggest that integrity is fidelity or conformity to righteousness. Someone who lives by integrity will be virtuous, decent, honorable, and upright. These words all describe someone who values truth and lives by a set of defined standards.

Oprah Winfrey has said that integrity is "doing the right thing, knowing that nobody's going to know whether you did it or not."[20] We are not born with integrity. It comes from the relentless pursuit of truth and honesty in one's life and is manifest regardless of the circumstances.

Integrity produces actions that are esteemed by others. It is similar to a reputation that must be earned. Our actions, not our words, demonstrate whether we have integrity.

Integrity cannot be faked. You can fake an image or reputation, because that is based on what other people think. You can hide behind a mask and display a false image that doesn't represent the real you. But integrity represents who you really are. You are either a person of integrity or you are not.

"Your image is what people think of you and your integrity is who you really are."
John Maxwell[21]

INTEGRITY IS A SHIELD

Righteousness and truth will shield you from deceit, gossip, slander, and many forms of evil. Honesty and truth will guard you from making critical mistakes. Your reputation of integrity will often cause those with shady intentions to steer clear of you. The key is having the internal ability to choose actions that are good, right, and honest. You cannot be dishonest and have integrity.

Integrity allows you to have a sense of calm and security, living without fear of lies being exposed and disrupting or even destroying your life.

Those who live with integrity also tend to have a family who honors and respects truth. There are great benefits in a family raised on honesty and integrity because the relationships in that family will be based on mutual trust. The children of parents living with integrity learn what is good or bad and right or wrong by observing the character of their parents. They live secure in the knowledge that honest lives are honored and respected by society.

Children who live in an atmosphere of truth will grow up in the knowledge that integrity matters. As adults they are safe and protected from the consequences of dishonesty.

Those who are dishonest and avoid the truth will become known and found out. Life for the dishonest is often not pleasant. Integrity will protect you from the consequences of a life built on dishonesty.

A person is not given integrity.
It is earned by the ongoing
and continual pursuit of honesty.

PEOPLE RESPECT INTEGRITY

People who act with integrity will be helped, either by authorities or by those who respect their moral or ethical character. People care for, help, and trust people of integrity. Why? Integrity produces actions, feelings, and emotions that draw others of like mind. People with integrity are thankful for help and will demonstrate appropriate gratitude to those who befriend them.

Hearing a good report about the character of someone of high integrity can be like money in the bank. People with integrity never have to talk about their own character because others will do it for them. If you are a parent and have received good reports from teachers about the character of your children, you know that your children are listening to your training and teaching.

Integrity will also lead to satisfaction and contentment. You cannot be content if your life is in chaos because of dishonesty or deceit. When your life is spent avoiding people to whom you have lied, formulating new lies, or getting others to lie to protect you, life is not comfortable or peaceful.

Integrity will draw people to your side and to your cause. Help and assistance is much easier to acquire when you live with integrity compared to the person that is untrustworthy. Why would people waste their time with people who are dishonest, are casual with the truth, and care little for doing what is right?

> *"Integrity without truth is worthless.*
> *Truth without integrity is a lie."*
> (Unknown)

RICH OR POOR

There are many wise sayings proclaiming that it is far better to be honest and poor than be rich and burdened with lying lips. Liars are frequently considered fools by their friends and the community in which they live. Rich men who live in deceit and dishonesty are without respect and frequently are dishonored by those around them.

But, whether you are rich or poor will not determine whether you live with integrity.

Wisdom suggests that even living in poverty is far better than living a comfortable life because of foolish behavior, deceit, double-dealing, fraud, or cheating. Producing a comfortable living through dishonesty and fraud does not make one's life joyful, satisfied, or content.

Money can sometimes hide perversity and deceit for a time, but it cannot cover serious dishonesty forever. The person who is a cheat eventually finds it hard to live with that knowledge. He lives with guilt and mistrust and tends to think everyone is trying to cheat him.

Being dishonest, a liar, and one who ignores truth creates various problems:

- A liar lives in stress, mountains of lies, distrust, guilt, and even fear.
- A liar's relationships with other people will be difficult to maintain.
- A liar will be burdened with shame.
- A bad reputation will cause serious problems for one trying to provide for a family.
- A liar will not be considered for opportunities because he will be viewed as unreliable.

Can you imagine how it might feel to be eating rich foods, wearing nice clothes, and living in a beautiful house, all because you are living off your dishonesty and the suffering of others? There can be very little true satisfaction or contentment in that life.

> *"Perhaps the surest test of an individual's integrity is his refusal to do or say anything that would damage his self-respect."*
> Thomas S. Monson[22]

TIPS FOR LIVING A LIFE OF INTEGRITY

Use these tips to help improve your integrity:

- Be cautious what you say on social media.
- Communicate promises clearly so there is no misunderstanding.
- Don't make promises you can't keep.
- Associate with other people of integrity.
- Establish integrity-related core values.
- Put your integrity above self-esteem. Be humble.
- Be accountable for what you do. Admit mistakes.

- Give grace to others when they struggle living a life of integrity.
- Listen and learn from correction or rebuke.
- Be willing to change.
- Overcome pride if it impacts your ability to live with integrity.
- Do not cheat on anything, big or small.

Liars must have excellent memories.
How is your memory?

TIPS YOU COULD USE

a. Underline, circle, or highlight the 1 to 3 tips above that you think could make the most impact if you implemented them in your life. You will revisit these choices at the end of the book in the Planning section.

b. There may be other things that you think would make a difference. Write them below:

_____

_____

_____

Wisdom to Action Challenge

Think about a recent decision you made. Did it align with your values and reflect your true character? Identify one action you can take this week to reinforce your commitment to integrity and live more authentically.

Chapter 6
COMPROMISE

"All compromise is based on give and take,
but there can be no give and take on fundamentals.
Any compromise on mere fundamentals is a surrender.
For it is all give and no take."
Mahatma Gandhi[23]

"A compromise is the art of dividing a cake in such a way that
everyone believes he has the biggest piece."
Ludwig Erhard[24]

Compromise can be both good and bad. The bad compromise involves our values, character, and ethical standards. If you stand for the truth, claim to be loyal, swear to be trustworthy, but compromise your promises or standards, then compromise is bad and can even be evil. A wise saying suggests, "When you have to compromise yourself or your moral or ethical standards for the people around you, it's time to change the people around you."[25]

However, in settling disputes or negotiating contracts, compromise can be rewarded. In such situations the parties are making mutual concessions or accommodations in order to arrive at a mutually agreeable result. In such circumstances people make concessions in order to receive the benefit of a contractual agreement.

Dale Carnegie has said in his book, *How to Win Friends and Influence People,* "The highest levels of influence are reached when generosity and trustworthiness surround your behavior." Think about this statement as it relates to compromise. If you trusted someone and they were generous, meaning they were willing to give away something that was of valuable to them, would you also be willing to be generous and give up something of value?

It's pretty difficult to be a cut-throat negotiator with people who are both trustworthy and generous. Compromising with people of high character usually produces a win-win situation for both parties.

"Learn the wisdom of compromise,
for it is better to bend a little than to break."
(Anonymous)

There is a story in the Old Testament of the Bible that is very instructive concerning compromise. You may have heard the names "Shadrach, Meshach, and Abednego" even if you did not know the story about their lives. Daniel and his three Jewish friends were in captivity in Babylon at the time of King Nebuchadnezzar. The king appointed Shadrach, Meshach and Abednego to manage the province of Babylon.

Later, the King dedicated a statue to himself and declared that all people were to fall down and worship the gold statue. Shadrach, Meshach and Abednego refused to obey the king's order. When they were brought before the king they were asked why they wouldn't serve his gods and bow down to the golden statue. Their response was:

> *"Nebuchadnezzar, we don't need to give you an answer to this question. If the God we serve exists, then He can rescue us from the furnace of blazing fire, and He can rescue us from the power of you, the king. But even if He does not rescue us, we want you as king to know that we will not serve your gods or worship the gold statue you set up."*

These three young men were very special people in very trying times. They stood firm without hesitation and without confrontation. They had the courage to stand up to the king, and were confident enough to put their faith and lowly position up against the authority of a powerful leader. This does not mean they were not scared or even terrified. But they were not afraid to die for their principles if that was required.

What is important about this story? We can conclude that the three were totally committed to the truth as they knew it. They were completely ready to rely on their principles and beliefs regardless of what the king might do. They exhibited a level of courage and boldness that most of us would envy. There are several important lessons to learn from their story:

- Difficulties, struggles, and trials should not impact your commitment to the truth.

- You should not reject the truth just to save your life.

How would you compare your dedication to integrity to that of Shadrach, Meshach, and Abednego? What would it take in your life to have a commitment like this? Would you have been prepared to suggest a compromise with the king? Would you have suggested a compromise to the three friends?

> *"Many things are worse than defeat, and*
> *compromise with evil is one of them."*
> (Anonymous)

COMPROMISING CHARACTER

Why didn't Daniel's three friends consider some form of compromise? Were there accommodations or concessions that might have been possible for them that would have replaced the threat of death? Were there more workable solutions for the three men rather than facing a fiery furnace? For example:

> COMPROMISE #1: What if the three young men had thought they could avoid trouble by just playing along with the king. They wouldn't really worship the golden image even though they bowed down. But if they would compromise here, where else would they compromise? This compromise would have signaled to all that were watching that they were not committed to their beliefs.
>
> COMPROMISE #2: What if the three men had said to themselves that it was a decree of the king or a law of the land and thus they were obligated to obey the law? Do you think this is a valid excuse for

violating beliefs and core values? Is it acceptable to violate your values because of the decrees of a leader or because laws make the behavior lawful?

COMPROMISE #3: What if the three young men had agreed that they would do this just one time in this large gathering and then not come back to this place in the future? But what if the decree required robbery, murder, or child abuse? Would it be acceptable to do it just once if they knew they could avoid being asked to do it again?

COMPROMISE #4: What if the three young men thought that their momentary lapse in judgment would be forgiven, especially under these circumstances? In this story that would have amounted to testing God or testing the truth. Therefore, the question becomes, "How important is the truth? What would they be willing to give up or lose in order to maintain their beliefs and core values?"

"Compromise, while at times morally necessary or at least justifiable, is more often only the first permission for a person (or society) to begin a long downhill descent."
Dennis Prager[26]

COMPROMISE IN MAKING AGREEMENTS

The art of compromise is often the key to reaching reasonable agreements with others. For example, unions and employers negotiate and compromise regularly in order to get the best deal for their constituents. The ability to compromise in this manner is considered a proper and appropriate means to produce working relationships that both parties can endorse.

However, if we compromise our word or our values, we will normally be looked upon with scorn and distrust by friends, co-workers, and even enemies. Our reputations can be permanently damaged resulting in others losing respect for us. People whose word cannot be trusted will find life difficult. Trying to be the best you can be while being untrustworthy is probably impossible.

Alternatively, if we won't compromise on less important or non-critical issues, we are often considered hardheaded, stubborn, and obstinate.

> *"All compromise is based on give and take,*
> *but there can be no give and take on fundamentals.*
> *Any compromise on mere fundamentals is surrender.*
> *For it is all give and no take."*
> Mahatma Gandhi[27]

STANDING FIRM

How do we stand firm? To some extent the degree to which we are committed to our goals, principles, or plans will determine how we react to pressure to reject or ignore our values. If we are not really committed, then we are likely to give in to early difficulties, peer pressure, or self-doubt. The best advice is to be prepared. If you know it's going to rain in the middle of a hike, you take rain gear.

Personal growth is no different. If you know temptation is going to occur or peer pressure will be unleashed when you refuse to participate in some activity, be prepared. Know in advance what you are going to say and do in those circumstances.

Avoid places and that will cause you to challenge your principles and values.

TIPS FOR STANDING FIRM

<u>WHAT TO DO:</u>

1. Do not be frightened by fools who might oppose you.
2. Expect opposition from people who do not hold your same values.

> This may be verbal in nature, and depending on the particular issue may be accompanied by threats to leave a group or cancel relationships. And, that may be for the best!

3. Don't waste time with people or activities that are opposed to your core values.
4. Be grateful and do everything without grumbling, complaining, or arguing.
5. Avoid fools, naysayers, and tempting bribes.
6. Ignore pleas of friends (peer pressure).
7. Don't rely totally on yourself. Have people of character who will support you.
8. Keep your eyes on the goal. Don't look back.

<u>HOLD FAST TO HIGH CHARACTER TRAITS:</u>

1. Live in harmony with those who hold to your values.
2. Be humble. Do not consider yourself better than others.
3. Be selfless, thankful, and generous.
4. Be gracious and look out for the needs of others.
5. Stand firm even in the face of ugly circumstances.
6. Hold onto your core values.[28]

One of the common characteristics of the suggestions above is that some form of action is required. Standing firm requires more than crossing our arms and staring down the enemy with a scowl. We cannot be sitting in our easy chairs in front of the TV if we need to marshal forces necessary to stand firm. Be ready and alert when your character is at stake, because action is necessary. Doing little or nothing probably means we have lost the battle.

TIPS YOU COULD USE

a. Underline, circle, or highlight the 1 to 3 tips above that you think could make the most impact if you implemented them in your life. You will revisit these choices at the end of the book in the Planning section.

b. There may be other things that you think would make a difference. Write them below:

_____

_____

_____

_____

"If you have integrity nothing else matters.
If you don't have integrity nothing else matters."
Alan K. Simpson[29]

Wisdom to Action Challenge

Consider a situation where you compromised. Did it involve your core values? Identify one area where you need to set stronger boundaries to protect your integrity, and commit to upholding those boundaries this week.

Chapter 7
Absolute Truth

"People will generally accept facts as truth
only if the facts agree with what they already believe."
Andy Rooney[30]

Absolute truth does exist! But many either believe it does not exist or they are confused over the definition and meaning. Merriam-Webster defines truth as (1) sincerity in action, character, and utterance; (2) the state or case of being a fact; (3) the body of real things, events, and facts, and (4) the property of being in accord with fact or reality.

Absolute truth is described as fact with no restriction, exception, or qualification. Josh McDowell defined absolute truth as that which is true for all people, for all times, in all places. It is something that is unequivocally true.[31]

Absolute truth is the same today
as it was yesterday and as it will be tomorrow.

HOW DOES SOCIETY DEFINE TRUTH?

Let's first note several important definitions from
MERRIAM-WEBSTER:

TRUTH: being in accord with facts or reality; accurate; in accord with the actual state of affairs.

HONESTY: truthful; free from fraud or deception; not lying, stealing, or cheating.

INTEGRITY: being honest and fair; strict adherence to a code of moral values; virtuous.

LYING: marked by untruth; false statement; and dishonesty.

CHEATING: to break a rule or law to gain advantage; to gain by lying; scam; swindle; fraud.

Traditionally, Europe and the western world have determined their moral rules or principles from the Judeo-Christian Ethic. Certainly that is true of the United States. Our founding fathers openly based our constitution and laws on an ethical standard established by a higher power.

Today, however, truth is viewed in several different ways. People who view truth in the following ways do not necessarily know these definitions, but what they believe falls into the following categories:

Pragmatism says there is no absolute truth, rather, truth lies solely in practical results. It is determined by experience and the consequences of things.

Subjectivism says truth is one's subjective reaction, experience, or response to occurrences. Thus, if a tree fell in the deep forest but no one saw it fall, the tree did not really fall.

Relativism says that truth is relative; man is the judge of what is right or wrong. Because there is no revelation from a higher source (God), there is no one to sit in judgment of man's mistakes. Therefore the Christian definition, or any other profound pronouncement, must be altered as necessary to be acceptable to man.

From the previous sentence you can see that there would be tension between those who accept absolute truth as set forth in the Bible and those who believe truth is relative and absolute truth does not exist. The Bible says truth is generated by a higher source and teaches that man must be transformed by that truth. The nature of truth is not changed to suit man, as is the case in *relativism*.

You may be wondering why this is important. What does it matter if people want to determine their own truth? In some cases you and I could just ignore the issue and let those who want to argue about it waste their time. But it is particularly important for us as we examine good character. What makes character "good"? Or, what makes something right or wrong? You might say it is bad if it is behavior that is against the law. But what if there were no man-made laws? What if all the laws were cancelled? What, then, makes something right, wrong, good, or bad?

For our purposes, the important characteristic is that values have been established by an outside source. Man himself did not determine right or wrong. If man is allowed to determine what is good and what is bad, the world will relatively quickly slide into anarchy and chaos. Man is inherently flawed and not capable of determining ethical principles, unless it personally suits him to do so. If man can determine his own ethical principles, then he can also change them when it suits him.

We say all this to demonstrate that our desire to be the very best we can be must be linked to the historic values of good and bad. Therefore, attractive and desirable personal characteristics include honesty, integrity, respect, honor, loyalty, and being trustworthy.

We will not spend any additional time arguing that the personal characteristics we are investigating are good or bad. Honesty and integrity are to be desired and evil, wickedness, deceit, un-forgiveness, pride, and greed are to be rejected! We accept the historical determination of what is right, wrong, good, and bad.

Wisdom to Action Challenge

Reflect on how absolute truth guides your decisions. How can you better align your actions with timeless principles? Identify one ethical decision you will face this week, and commit to making it based on unwavering truth.

Chapter 8
TRUTH

"The truth doesn't always set you free;
people prefer to believe prettier, neatly wrapped lies"
Jodi Picoult[33]

WHY TRUTH IS IMPORTANT

Why does truth matter? Dishonesty will cause most people a great deal of distress. This occurs because one becomes ashamed or feels guilty about their behavior. Guilt is a big factor in living with the stain of dishonesty. There is also the ongoing stress of keeping the lies alive and the worry of being found out.

Being untruthful is not a good habit. The person who allows the practice of lying to become a habit will eventually discover that it is a very hard habit to break. Liars have great difficulty in maintaining relationships and lying on the job is an excellent way to find yourself looking for a new job. Truth is fundamental to having high character. It cannot be achieved without a commitment to honesty.

The person who gains a reputation for being a liar, will find that reputation very difficult to live down. Even if he overcomes the bad behavior, the trust that has been lost is extremely hard to restore. Obviously, it's best not to go down that road at all. Make honesty and integrity a foundation of your character. Avoid the embarrassment of needing to fix a bad reputation by making truth and integrity the cornerstones of your core values.

Decide that you will always tell the truth, regardless of the difficulty it may cause you. It may require courage, but the alternative is a lie that will eventually be discovered and your character will be revealed. The truth may make someone unhappy, even angry, but the alternative is worse.

Speak the truth in love with a gentle and humble spirit. If someone is hurt or upset with that truth, it means they want to perpetuate a lie caused by their own inadequacies or mistakes. That is not your fault or your problem. The suggestion that a friend would lie to protect them is nonsense and illogical.

You cannot shade the truth. It is either true or it is not. If you claim something is true, but it is only true 90% of the time, then it's not true. This is a concept that many people struggle with. Absolute truth does exist. Something does not become untrue simply because someone chooses not to believe it or because they claim it to be untrue. And something does not become true just because someone declares it to be true.

Truth is sincere and genuine. It does not vary based on exterior circumstances. It is a fact; the state of being actual or existing in reality. When Joe Friday of the old TV show "Dragnet" interviewed witnesses to crimes, he would say, "Give me the facts Ma'am, just the facts." Truth represents the facts, and just the facts. It is free from deceit, fraud, deception, trickery, fakery, or delusion.

People of character detest dishonesty. These are very strong words. But they are true: people of character and truth loathe liars, cheaters, and all things deceitful. They view liars with disgust and mistrust. Have you ever thought in terms of abhorring something? Are people with these high principles just being picky? No. There are no degrees of dishonestly. You are either dishonest and a cheater or you are not.

> *"One word of truth outweighs the whole world."*
> Alexander Solzhenitsyn[34]

VALUE TRUTH

Friends and business associates take great pleasure in honest people. They value others who speak the truth and act in truth. Leaders in particular value honesty. Leaders cannot lead or govern alone. Either citizens must be trustworthy or the army who oppresses them must be trustworthy. Even evil kings must depend on the honesty and loyalty of other people.

Honesty has been described like a kiss on the lips, because it is so desirable it can be compared to the passion of a lover's kiss. You can trust those who are honest with almost anything. But those who are deceitful are not honest, trustworthy, dependable, or reliable. They are deceptive, fraudulent, and cheaters. You cannot trust them. Therefore, a relationship is not viable with such people.

Do you have any friends or associates whom you would consider deceitful? Do they think you value truth and honesty? If not, why not? Do you value their relationship? Why?

Truth and honesty can shield one from many pitfalls and wrong turns. Truth will protect you from the consequences associated with dishonesty.

The key to successful living is committing yourself to honesty and then intentionally choosing to do what is right, even when it appears shading the truth could benefit you.

The honest person chooses what is right, regardless.

VALUE THE INTEGRITY OF FRIENDS

There is a wise saying that says honesty and integrity can always be trusted, while the words of an enemy are never reliable. Just like the sales pitch of a slick salesman, we are inclined to question anything they say about their product. However, we completely trust the words of friends who have proven their integrity.

What if you had no friends or associates you could trust to tell you the brutal truth, when necessary? It is wise to accept the exhortation, correction, or rebuke of a friend you trust. Why? Because they have your best interests at heart and will tell you the truth, even if it is distasteful.

If you don't have such a friend, then who do you trust to give you accurate advice, a stranger or an enemy? I'll choose a friend who will tell me the truth, even if I don't like it. Enemies love to flatter people of influence. They use flattery, lies, and deceit to influence your behavior. But the words of a friend can be trusted.

> *"Nearly all men can stand adversity,*
> *but if you want to test a man's character,*
> *give him power."*
> Abraham Lincoln[35]

TRUTH ENDURES

How do you feel about people you know who lie or are dishonest? Do you want to associate with them or do business with them? Typically you cannot trust liars under any circumstances, because you never know when they are speaking lies or truth.

Truth is everlasting, but lies last only until they are found out. What does it mean that truth endures and lies do not? Falsehoods and lies are generally found out very quickly, producing hurt and trouble. But truth will last because it is true and does not change. Truth lasts – time does not change truth. What is true today is true tomorrow. Lies have to be replaced by more lies and different lies to sustain their delusion.

If something is true and the circumstances don't change, it will be true next month, next year, and even next century. History is like truth in that regard. The fact that Columbus sailed to America or slaves were imported like cattle from Africa are true today, no matter how distasteful the facts may be. The holocaust did happen and no amount of cover up or subterfuge will change the facts. Mistakes in the past should teach us lessons, not be altered or covered up.

The truth is the truth, is the truth, is the truth . . .

TRUTH CAN BE DANGEROUS

Can truth really be dangerous? This statement was probably not true a hundred years ago, but life has changed dramatically in the last fifty years. For example, today you may be held accountable for the truth and have to publically demonstrate that something is true.

You can be shamed, rejected, and ignored for your position supporting the truth, and all the logical arguments in the world will not change the minds of certain opponents. In today's society we find people who attack the speaker personally in an attempt to discredit the truth.

Depending on the nature of the situation you might be tempted to lie other than face the consequences of the truth. Thus, lies become accepted as truth because the problem of discrediting the lies is either dangerous or extremely time consuming or expensive. It simply becomes easier to ignore the lie. This often produces apathy on the part of those who know the truth. If you are one who prefers to avoid conflict and not to confront lies, you may find a commitment to honesty and integrity very difficult at times.

If you compromise the truth, you are likely to compromise other related character traits. If you are afraid of what others think it will be challenging for you to tell the truth, because there will always be people who disagree with you because they do not like the truth.

*Truth and its implications today are not
what they were only several generations ago.
Choose your words carefully!*

Your words are extremely important in this day and age when truth is often marginalized in favor of political, business, and personal agendas. Therefore, even when you tell the truth, if it conflicts with someone else's agenda, you can find yourself ridiculed and attacked, and even fired from your job. You may even be forced to defend your view of the truth. People today have little tolerance and think they can do and say anything in order to push their own agendas.

Therefore, it is important that you are both truthful and careful how you tell that truth. You must choose your words carefully.

It seems illogical that we should be as concerned about speaking the truth as we are about being dishonest. Consequences of lies vary with the nature of the lie. You can cause great damage with a small lie. But the size of the damage is generally related to the size of the lie. Again, it is important to choose your words carefully. The truth is always the best choice in any situation.

There are a number of good outcomes produced by telling the truth. The truthful person will:

- acquire a good reputation,
- have a good self-image,
- not need to worry about being discovered,

- not need to remember past lies,
- be able to live free of stress, and
- not hurt others because of lies.

TIPS FOR TELLING THE TRUTH

1. TEN REASONS TO TELL THE TRUTH

1. It helps those around you grow in their understanding.
2. It gives you peace and satisfaction.
3. It demonstrates you care.
4. It builds and supports your reputation.
5. It assists in building meaningful relationships.
6. It allows communication because without trust effective communication is nearly impossible.
7. Lies accomplish no purpose.
8. Lies ultimately make a situation worse.
9. Lies may mask a more serious situation that should be addressed.
10. Lies seldom remain a secret.

2. TEN WAYS TO BE EFFECTIVE

1. Take adequate time to know exactly what you want to say. Don't rush to speak.
2. When delivering bad news, be confident, gentle, and caring. Use a calm tone and don't be aggressive or accusatory.
3. Make sure your motives are pure and appropriate.
4. Be very specific and clear, leaving no room for misunderstanding. Write out your words if necessary.

5. Follow up to clarify. Put it in writing so that it cannot be misunderstood.

6. The truth is not always easy to tell or hear, so be prepared for questions and feedback.

7. Tell the good with the bad.

8. If you are not sure if you should speak, remain silent.

9. Ask for help in understanding the discussion. Don't make the situation worse by not understanding the facts. Get clarification if necessary.

10. Speak your peace and stop. Don't ramble on trying to explain or elaborate.

3. HELP YOUR CHILDREN TELL THE TRUTH

1. Provide positive reinforcement for telling the truth.

2. Be a role model. Allow your child to learn by watching you.

3. Make truth a family rule. Stress the importance of integrity and truthful communication.

4. Give warnings. Depending on the age and situation, giving one warning is usually appropriate.

5. Determine the reason and nature of the lie. Young children often tell fantasy lies. Why are they boasting? Do they want attention? Do they feel inadequate? They may be trying to avoid punishment. Children must learn that lying does not pay.

6. Lying should incur greater consequence. If you normally require a "timeout," add a loss of some privilege for lying. Children must quickly learn that lying has serious consequences.

7. Discuss the importance of honesty with your children. No lie is acceptable. Children can begin to understand the difference between lies and truth between the ages of 3-5. Discuss the possible consequences of lying.[36]

TIPS I COULD USE

a. Underline, circle, or highlight the 1 to 3 tips above that you think could make the most impact if you implemented them in your life. You will revisit these choices at the end of the book in the Planning section.

b. There may be other things that you think would make a difference. Write them below:

_____

_____

_____

_____

Wisdom to Action Challenge

Evaluate your daily interactions. Are you consistently truthful in your words and actions? Identify one area where you can practice greater honesty, and commit to speaking the truth, even in uncomfortable situations.

Chapter 9

WRAP-UP

Honesty produces contentment and satisfaction.
There is no contentment in dishonesty,
bad behavior, deceit, or evil.
We must both speak the truth and then act it out.

THE FOCUS

Remember, the goal is to be honest, live with integrity, and base our life on truth.

We have discussed a number of aspects of truth and honesty and how they would impact our lives. It is our position that if you concentrate on this principle, all the other aspects of good character will be much easier to achieve because they are built on the foundation of truth and honesty.

For example, honesty, integrity, and truth will:

- produce a good self-image and lead to confidence.
- cause one to be sincere and genuine.
- mean that one is responsible.
- result in respect and a good reputation.

The above are just a few of the character traits where honesty, integrity, and truth are the foundation to other traits. This demonstrates their critical importance in our lives and how fundamental they are to our well-being.

WINNING

Some believe life is a contest and they must use any and all actions to win. Therefore being devious or deceptive is acceptable behavior because the goal is to come out on top. These people are often very competitive and they may not be concerned how they win, as long as they win. Their attitude is often to win at all costs. They may not even think of their activities as competition, but simply the normal game of life.

But what do you think happens between you and your "opponent" if you win some contest, negotiation, or business client because you were deceptive or under-handed? You quickly lose trust! Your opponent will never want to deal with or play with you again. You will never be a friend.

Once your attitudes and reputation are made known, your reputation can be destroyed. Crafty and deceptive people are often hated (or at least greatly disliked). Their competitive nature makes them unwelcome associates.

You may wonder why you shouldn't use everything at your disposal to beat business rivals, sports opponents, school rivals, or those you are competing with for the next career promotion. Isn't being smart a virtue?

Yes, but being cagy, devious, or cunning is not a virtue except in the eyes of other schemers. Being smart and shrewd are virtues if they are used in a good way, aboveboard, and not to gain unfair advantage by being sly, or dodgy. If you are confused or unsure of what to do, ask yourself, "How would I feel if what I am about to do would be done to me?"

"There is no better test of a man's integrity than his behavior when he is wrong."
Marvin Williams[37]

BE CONTANTLY ON GUARD

I have a friend who works in a large corporation that periodically holds retreats or in-house training seminars for their employees. Being in middle management he is often asked to attend. At one training session the entire group was split into twenty teams of approximately 8 people. Each team was paired against another team. One team was given a sum of money that varied from $20 to $1000. The other team was told that the amount was between $20 and $1000, but not the actual amount. The two teams were to come together and negotiate how to split the money between the two groups. The two teams would be allowed to keep the money and split it individually between the members of each group based on the negotiation agreement.

My friend was on the team that got the money. He assumed the negotiations for their group and concocted a deceptive story that convinced the other team that the total amount they had been given was $75 when in fact it was $400. Obviously the people on his team were happy because they each walked away with some real money, but the other team was not pleased when they found out they had been duped.

But this was only a game, right? Maybe, but on Monday morning the winning group had to go back to work with those who felt they had been cheated. My friend commented that it took a long time before trust could be reestablished between members of the two groups. Was the deception worth it? No. The interesting thing about this story is that the people in the winning group were not inherently deceptive people, but were easily manipulated by money and competition.

We must be constantly on guard. No one in the winning group stopped to think about the consequences. No one considered the impact on their reputations.

THE INTEGRITY LIFE PRINCIPLE

There are many benefits to adopting the Integrity Life Principle. Honesty and integrity will provide an atmosphere that draws others to your side or group. It will allow effective groups to form around you because people will trust the environment in the group. Honestly allows the group to be sincere and focused on the goal at hand rather than on protecting personal agendas.

Truth telling produces the courage for others to offer their truth and perspective on questions, projects, ideas, and even relationships. If opposing views are discouraged, truth will often be masked in platitudes and flattery.

There are no negative consequences for being open and truthful. People will be open and true when they experience others who display openness with integrity. There is no reason to be closed and protective if a group honors those who tell the truth.

Honesty is the foundation for true relationships. Integrity is an open invitation for others to join your circle of associates. People with similar core values will support each other in both times of stress and success. If you are true, sincere, and genuine, you will attract others who are trustworthy. Truth is a magnet for people seeking friends or co-workers they can trust.

When you live with integrity your life can be calm and you can be at peace because you have no fear of consequences from dishonesty or reprisal because of lies. You can live confidently that your days will not be disrupted by the discovery of lies or deceit.

WALK THE TALK

If you claim to live with integrity then what do you do when you make mistakes? Do you admit them and move to a solution or do you make excuses and try to shift blame to others? When you make promises do you always intend to keep them or are you only trustworthy when it is convenient? Can people trust you when you say you will do something? Are you dependable and reliable?

What about the secrets you hear from your co-workers, friends, and associates? Do you keep them secret or do you use them when it is advantageous for your own purposes? Do you tend to boast about the work you do? Do you ever overstate the value of your work or your contribution? If you tend to brag about good work, do you also speak about the failures?

How interested or concerned are you about the work, projects, or relationships of others? Do you show genuine interest or are you in a competition? Do you really want your friends to succeed? Do you respond in a positive or negative manner depending on whether or not you are being observed by other people? Do you speak and act differently when people are watching?

If you have core values, do you religiously adhere to them? Do your friends know what your core values are? What happens if and when you break a core value? What happens if someone criticizes your work or what you say? How do you respond? How often do you find it necessary to tell social lies? Why?

Life is much easier when you walk the talk.

Think before you act. Your reputation is important!

Wisdom to Action Challenge

Think about how honesty and integrity shape your character. Identify one area where you can strengthen your commitment to these values, and take concrete steps to reinforce them in your daily life.

Chapter 10
Planning Part 1
Life Analysis

INTEGRITY LIFE PRINCIPLE:

Be honest, live with integrity, and base your life on truth.

INTRODUCTION

The objective of this Life Analysis chapter is to survey your life situation for information that will be used in later chapters to identify your core values, life priorities, commitments, and goals. In Chapter 13 we will formulate action steps to make being honest, living with integrity, and basing your life on truth a reality in your life.

If you have already read one of the other books in this series and completed the Life Analysis in that book, the questions and exercises are the same, but, your answers are about a different subject. However, some of your responses will be the same or similar and you might want to have that book handy as you complete this Life Analysis.

Most of us have never done any kind of extensive self-examination and certainly not thought about writing down the results. I can tell you personally there is much to be gained from writing them down rather than just thinking, talking, or meditating about them. It will give you a clear picture of your life and help you evaluate what you really want to accomplish.

The focus of this book is to address <u>one</u> particular topic in your life. It is not a complete life plan. A complete and detailed Life Plan is the subject of our *Life Planning Handbook*. See the "Next Steps" page at the end of this book for more information.

Our life planning process has five primary parts which we will cover in the following chapters.

Chapter 10, Part 1 – Life Analysis: What is your life situation today?
Chapter 11, Part 2 – Life Values: What is important to you?
Chapter 12, Part 3 – Life Principle Goals: What are your objectives?
Chapter 13, Part 4 – Action Steps: How do you get from where you are today to your goals?
Chapter 14, Part 5 – Ongoing Progress Review: How are you doing?

Life planning is not a difficult process. It will certainly be easier for those who have thought about these questions before. You might even have an existing plan of some kind. If so, this will be a good check on where you are and how you are doing. If you have a plan, it would be worthwhile pulling it out as you progress through the remaining parts of this book.

"If you don't know where you're going,
any path will get you there!"

I don't know the source of this quote but I have had it emblazoned in my brain since my college days. I think it came from one of my college business classes or textbooks. I have heard it repeated a number of times over the years, primarily because it is so true.

If you don't know your destination, then any choice of roads at all the forks in life will be an acceptable choice. It won't really matter which road you take because you don't have a destination in mind anyway. And when you get there you won't know you have arrived.

We need a purpose, a destination, and priorities so we are not wandering aimlessly through life. Even if you are not a "planning person," be assured we will walk you through every step. Knowing your path is important because:

    1) Every path leads somewhere.

    2) The life-road on which you are traveling, the direction in which you are heading, and your expected destination <u>will</u> determine your life.

    3) You cannot allow apathy, other people, or chance to determine either your path or your destination.

Without purpose and direction it is difficult to make good choices. Just thinking about the questions we will ask in the following process will be helpful. Our planning process should produce these positive results:

- it will create focus, attention, and desire,

- it will cause action – doing something,
- it will establish what you believe,
- it will help you make better decisions,
- it will help reduce distractions and hindrances, and
- it will motivate you.

"Perhaps the surest test of an individual's integrity
is his refusal to do or say anything
that would damage his self-respect."
Thomas S. Monson[38]

LIFE ANALYSIS – KNOW YOURSELF

The first step in any form of life planning is to know and understand where you are today. What is your current situation? What is impacting your decisions and ultimately your life today? The first objective will be to identify your present situation and circumstances. Before we begin, take note of the following suggestions:

1. During this process you may find that you draw a blank on a particular question. If that happens, move on to the next question and return to the unanswered ones at a later time.

2. These questions relate specifically to the Integrity Life Principle which is focused on honesty, integrity, and truth. If that limited scope makes it

difficult to answer any particular question, then answer from a broader life perspective if you think it would be helpful. If the question doesn't apply in any significant way, leave it blank.

3. You might find it convenient to write your initial responses in a separate notebook or computer and transfer that information to this book after you have thought about it and modified it to accurately reflect your thoughts and circumstances.
Regardless of how you develop your answers, keep your notes, as they may be useful at a later date.

4. Remember, you are developing a plan focused on the Integrity Life Principle, not on your life in general. Therefore, your responses should be focused on that subject.

KNOW YOURSELF – Interests

INSTRUCTION: What are the things and activities you love to do? What gives you joy as related to the Integrity Life Principle?

1.

_____

2.

_____

3.

_____

4.

_____

5.

_____

KNOW YOURSELF – Skills

INSTRUCTION: What are your greatest physical or mental skills and abilities related to the Integrity Life Principle?

1.

_____

2.

_____

3.

_____

4.

_____

5.

_____

KNOW YOURSELF – Strengths

INSTRUCTION: What are your strengths, special skills, and passions in regard to the Integrity Life Principle?

1.

_____

2.

_____

3.

_____

4.

_____

5.

_____

KNOW YOURSELF – Weaknesses

INSTRUCTION: What are your weaknesses in regard to the Integrity Life Principle?

1.

_____

2.

_____

3.

_____

4.

_____

5.

_____

KNOW YOURSELF – Roadblocks

Who or what things do you fear the most? What are the roadblocks, distractions, and hindrances that might prevent you from improving your life in any way?

Circle any that might apply and add your own in the empty boxes.

Disabilities	Failure	Bankruptcy	Divorce	Loss of job
Public speaking	Confrontation	War	Loss of friends	Peer pressure
Poor health	My boss	Guilt	No legacy	God
Time	Apathy	Relationships	Death	Family
Inability to stand firm	Immoral behavior	Unethical behavior	Lack of skills and abilities	Emotions and feelings
Fears and insecurities	Lack purpose in life	Lack of Core values	Lack of patience	Improper motives
Bad habits				

INSTRUCTION: Based on what you circled above, record any <u>serious</u> roadblocks or hindrances that could prevent you from achieving the Integrity Life Principle. Indicate the reason they are roadblocks.

1.

_____

2.

_____

3.

_____

4.

_____

KNOW YOURSELF – Character

How would you evaluate your personal character? Do you have any serious character flaws (your religious friends might refer to these as sins)? If you have any serious character flaws in your life, you may need to deal with them in order to make real progress toward your Integrity Life Principle objectives.

INSTRUCTION: Circle the positive traits which you lack and the existence of character flaws that might hinder your ability to achieve the Integrity Life Principle.

LACK OF POSITIVE CHARACTER TRAITS:				
Honesty	Kindness	Caring	Forgiving	Goodness
Hopeful	Humility	Dependable	Loving	Diligence
Respectful	Godly	Patient	Generous	Satisfied
Peace	Merciful	Trustworthy	Self-controlled	Thankful
Devout	Discipline	Obedient	Gentle	Prudent
Sincerity	Fair/Just	Grateful		
EXISTING CHARACTER FLAWS:				
Bad language	Boastfulness	Gossip	Slanderous	Lying
Cheating	Stubbornness	Anger	Hostility	Fear
Foolishness	Mischievousness	Rebellion	Hypocrisy	Envy
Unruliness	Ingratitude	Pride	Immorality	Addictions
Jealousy	Bitterness	Hatred	Unforgiving	Shame
Respecy	Deceitfulness	Deceit	Vanity	Revenge

The above list is not exhaustive. If there are other issues you should add, write them in the empty boxes above.

INSTRUCTION: Review the issues you have identified and list anything below that could seriously hinder achieving the Integrity Life Principle. List the issue and how it would negatively impact your ability to achieve your objectives.

1.

_____

_____

2.

_____

_____

3.

_____

_____

KNOW YOURSELF – Conclusion

This concludes your information gathering. You should now have at your fingertips a good overview of who you are and what might impact your ability to achieve the Integrity Life Principle, both good and bad.

The next step in the process of knowing yourself is to use this information to determine your core values, life priorities, and life commitments.

Chapter 11

Planning Part 2
Life Values

——

INTEGRITY LIFE PRINCIPLE:

Be honest, live with integrity, and base your life on truth.

CORE VALUES

What are the standards by which you live? What values do you cherish? What do you believe in? What values or standards will you absolutely not compromise or violate? The latter are your *core values*.

Self-assessment and full understanding of yourself and your environment must begin with identifying and knowing your core values. Core values are the principles, standards, or beliefs that are so important to you that you would not violate them. They will dictate your most important decisions and help you choose your direction.

You don't need to have your whole life figured out, but you do need to know what matters most to you. You need to know your ethical and moral standards. What issues or actions do you believe in so strongly that you would be deeply ashamed if you violated them? These are values and principles you believe in and live by, and to the best of your ability you will not forsake them. They represent who you really are. They are your core values.

If you are a religious person you might have a core value that indicates you would stand firm on your religious principles, and you might name them. If you love and seek intellectual improvement you might have a core value related to seeking and gaining knowledge and wisdom. If you are a dedicated parent you probably have core values related to your children or parenting.

Some core values may change or become more or less important as you age and the path of your life journey changes.

You may be aware of several of your core values but you probably have never written them down. This exercise will be an important step in understanding yourself and what is important to you.

If this is a new subject for you, you might start by looking at all the topics on the "Life Planning Series" page (prior to Chapter 1) and determine if any of those subjects represent core values for you. There are other subjects that might be appropriate for you to consider, for example: wisdom, influence, health, leadership, security, fitness, family, volunteer service, ethics, joy, relationships, moderation, balance, justice/injustice, addictions, laws, safety, etc.

Your core values should cover the things that are important to you. For example, you might have a core value of: "I will always try to do what is right and I will teach my children to do what is right, even if it is uncomfortable." Or, you might have a core value related to money: "I will never spend more than I earn. I will pay off credit cards monthly."

FINAL CORE VALUES

Develop these values based on a total life perspective, not just the Integrity Life Principle, and make them work for you. If you have never thought about this before, we recommend you begin with 5 to 8, but no more than 12. This is a critical step in this planning exercise, so spend sufficient time thinking and evaluating your final choices. Remember, core values are those values or standards that you will absolutely not compromise or violate.

INSTRUCTION: Develop your list of core values and record them here. We suggest you try to list twelve and then cut the list back to the best 5 to 8.

1. _____

2. _____

3. _____

4. _____

5. _____

6. _____

7. _____

8. _____

9. _____

10. _____

11. _____

12. _____

Do any of the core values you listed above relate to honesty, integrity, or truth? If not, do you need one? You may not, but don't leave it off because you overlooked the obvious. You may want to include one in order to give your objectives for the Integrity Life Principle more focus and importance at this time.

LIFE VALUES: Priorities (initial list)

Our perspective in this exercise is your total life, not just the Integrity Life Principle.

What are the things that are very important to you today? What are your life priorities? Where do you currently spend your money and your time? What do you spend your life doing and thinking about? For this initial list of priorities, ignore anything new that you may be considering relative to living a better life. Record just your priorities today (the good and the bad).

If you do something daily or regularly, then it is probably a priority. If you average more than an hour a day doing something, it's also probably a priority. What do you regularly spend money on? Assuming you have a normal

8:00 – 5:00 job, what do you do in the evenings and on weekends?

You might have Life Priorities related to your spiritual life, the educational system where you live, the ethical standards of your friends, your health and diet, hobbies and activities, raising your children, your marriage, your times of pleasure and relaxation, politics, volunteer service, your work ethic, saving money, immorality, your job or career, where you will live, your personal growth, etc.

INSTRUCTION: What are your actual top 6 to 12 life priorities today? Record them here based on a total life perspective.

1.
_____

2.
_____

3.
_____

4.
_____

5.
_____

6.
_____

7.
_____

8.
_____

9.

_____

10.

_____

11.

_____

12.

_____

ISSUES – URGENCY:

If you learned that you had only two years of life left, what impact would that have on your Life Priorities? How might they change?

_____

_____

_____

_____

_____

_____

ISSUES – SACRIFICES AND RISKS:

What new risks or sacrifices would you have to make in order to accomplish the Integrity Life Principle? Would that change your current Life Priorities?

_____

_____

_____

_____

_____

ISSUES – KNOWING YOURSELF:

Look back over the "Life Analysis – Know Yourself" and determine if there is anything that should change or be added to your Life Priorities.

_____

_____

_____

_____

_____

_____

ISSUES – LIVING A BETTER LIFE:

Given a desire to adopt the Integrity Life Principle for your life, what new priorities would you need to adopt? Ask yourself what you must absolutely do in order to successfully live a better life. What new priorities does that create and how would any existing priorities have to change?

_____

_____

_____

_____

_____

_____

_____

FINAL LIFE PRIORITIES

Prepare a complete list below of your new and revised total Life Priorities. Try to keep this list at 6 to 8, but no more than 12. You should intentionally include priorities that relate to the Integrity Life Principle.

1.

_____

2.

_____

3.

_____

4.

_____

5.

_____

6.

_____

7.

_____

8.

_____

9.

_____

10.

_____

11.

_____

12.

_____

LIFE COMMITMENTS

Are these Commitments the same as Life Priorities? No! Your Life Priorities identify the *things that are very important* to you, while Life Commitments are *things you must do* to make Life Priorities a reality in your life. Life Commitments are sometimes useful if they focus on areas where you have particular difficulties.

It's very possible that there are new commitments you must make that are not directly related to the Integrity Life Principle. For example, if your desire is to be honest you will also have to commit to being trustworthy, dependable, reliable, and loyal. If you want to be generous, then you can't love money. If you desire to guard your speech, then you cannot be out of control and let anger control your tongue. If you are going to live a life free of drugs, then you must commit to eliminating friends and associates who use drugs.

The point of these examples is to demonstrate that if you are serious about the Integrity Life Principle, then automatically there will be other related commitments necessary to be successful. You could have a commitment that says you are going to commit to being honest with everyone, but that doesn't really provide you with much help. If you commonly lie to your spouse, then a commitment to never lie to your spouse becomes a more meaningful commitment. If your difficulty with truth revolves around not keeping promises, you could commit to never making a promise you don't intend to keep. Try to make your commitments specific enough that they will be useful to you.

The important concept to recognize is that the Integrity Life Principle will *automatically* require committing to one or more other behaviors and traits that are related to integrity and may be troublesome if not an area of focus.

Since Life Priorities inherently identify your objectives, examine those priorities and determine the related commitments that you must make in order to achieve each Life Priority. The focus should be on what you must commit to in order to achieve the Integrity Life Principle.

INSTRUCTION: List the traits, behaviors, activities, or habits that you must manage or control in order for <u>you</u> to achieve the Integrity Life Principle (one or two words).

1. _____

2. _____

3. _____

4. _____

5. _____

6. _____

7. _____

8. _____

9. _____

10. _____

FINAL LIFE COMMITMENTS

INSTRUCTION: Based on the above, develop the Life Commitments you feel you should make in order to successfully achieve the Integrity Life Principle. These should be significant commitments, therefore, select the 4 to 8 that would really help you in living a life of integrity.

"There's a difference between interest and commitment.
When you are interested in doing something,
you do it only when it's convenient.
When you're committed to something,
you accept no excuses, only results."
Kenneth Blanchard[39]

1.

_____

_____

2.

_____

_____

3.

_____

_____

4.

_____

_____

INTEGRITY LIFE PRINCIPLE: Be honest, live with integrity, and base your life on truth.

5.

_____

_____

6.

_____

_____

7.

_____

_____

8.

_____

_____

Chapter 12

Planning Part 3
Life Goals

————

INTEGRITY LIFE PRINCIPLE

Be honest, live with integrity, and base your life on truth.

"Life takes on meaning when you become motivated,
set goals and charge after them
in an unstoppable manner."
Les Brown[40]

Our Life Goal in this book is the Integrity Life Principle: *I will be honest, live with integrity, and base my life on truth.* A complete plan would have other goals, but in this book we are focused only on one goal: honesty, integrity, and truth.

If it would be useful for you, you may want to note or record other important Life Goals you already have or you want to make given the material you have read in this book.

Life Goals are your objectives for the future. They are influenced by your Core Values, Life Priorities, and your Commitments.

LIFE GOALS

INSTRUCTION: We have entered the Integrity Life Principle goal, and you may list other personal goals, if you like.

1. *I will be honest, live with integrity, and base my life on truth.*

    <u>OTHERS (for future use):</u>

    2.
    _____

    3.
    _____

    4.
    _____

    5.
    _____

    6.
    _____

"Your ability to discipline yourself to set clear goals, and then to work toward them every day, will do more to guarantee your success than any other single factor."
Brian Tracy[41]

Chapter 13

Planning Part 4
Action Steps

——

INTEGRITY LIFE PRINCIPLE:
Be honest, live with integrity, and base your life on truth.

If you want something to happen,
you will need to take action.

INTRODUCTION

All the work in the previous chapters has given you a wealth of knowledge about where you are today and what you want to achieve in the future. You have even written it down. This is the point at which you actually take the step to determine what you are going to do about it.

As you think about what you need to do, include language that would allow you to measure your success or progress, if possible. Where appropriate, include the dates when you intend to begin and complete each step. The best action steps are those that can be measured, allowing you to easily evaluate your progress.

Another action step might include what would happen if you fail at keeping your commitments or priorities. Think in advance what you will do if you have a temporary lapse or failure of some kind. For example, if your goal is honesty, what will you do if you lie to someone? A possible action step might be to make a list of the things you could do after you catch yourself in a lie.

In most cases the Life Principle involved will dictate the nature of the action steps you will want to take. For example, if the goal is to be honest, having an action step that says, "I will never lie" is good but probably too general in nature. Think about specific situations that will likely arise for you where it would be easy to violate your integrity. You might begin by listing the people to whom you are most concerned about lying:

- spouse
- boss
- client
- friend(s)

If your primary issue of dishonesty is your boss, then only develop action steps for being truthful to your boss. When you develop your action steps, concentrate on the areas that cause you difficulty. Don't bother with areas where you don't really have a problem.

ACTION STEPS – FIRST DRAFT

Following is a list of subjects for developing your action steps. You can do all of them or just those that you expect will produce the results you want. Your ultimate objective is to end up with 4 to 6 action steps you intend to implement in your life. You will have other actions (maybe a large number) on your initial list, but the ultimate goal is 4 to 6 good steps that you are confident will have a significant impact on achieving your objectives.

IMPORTANT: Produce as many good ideas as possible in this initial listing process. They may be useful at a later date.

ACTION STEPS – Initial List

INSTRUCTION: Do each of the following in order to produce an initial list of actions steps for making the Integrity Life Principle a reality in your life. After you produce this initial list you will consolidate and remove the ideas that are not on target. We suggest doing this initial list in a separate notebook or on your tablet or computer.

Step #1 – TIPS FOR IMPROVEMENT

You have actually done much of the work for utilizing the tips we have discussed. In chapters 3 through 9 we provided tips on how you might improve a particular character trait. You were asked to highlight 1 to 3 suggestions you thought might work best for you and to list any other thoughts you had that would improve that trait.

Go back through the entire list of tips you chose and the ideas you added and select the ones you might actually want to use as action steps. Select the ones that would have the most positive impact on the Integrity Life Principle. Choose the best 4 to 12 tips, and write them in the space below in any order. [The tips are located on pages 27, 47, 53, 61, and 75].

TIPS:

1.

_____

2.

_____

3.

_____

4.

_____

5.

_____

6.

_____

7.

_____

8.

_____

9.

_____

10.

_____

11.

_____

12.

_____

CHOOSE THE BEST TIPS:

From the list above, choose the top 4 to 6 tips and list them in <u>priority</u> order:

1.

_____

2.

_____

3.

_____

4.

_____

5.

_____

6.

_____

Make one or more of these tips the first entries on your to your master list of Initial Action Steps.

Step #2 – IMPLEMENTATION TECHNIQUES

It will be helpful for you to think about implementation techniques before you begin determining your final action steps. These are techniques you can utilize to help you achieve your goals. You might automatically mentally use some of these concepts when you are developing and working your plan. But if they are not already second nature to you, they could be part of your action steps.

Be Intentional. If you are going to accomplish anything of value, change some part of your life, or achieve a goal, you will need both discipline and intentionality. Developing a plan and even writing down action steps will accomplish very little unless you actually follow through. You must be committed, disciplined, and intentionally do what's necessary.

Be open to change. Change is occurring daily all around us. If we are rigid and not open to new ways and new ideas, it is often difficult to accept good advice. For example, how can new ways to communicate help you be honest?

Seek knowledge and understanding. We cannot afford to be ignorant. Those with skills and expertise can teach us much. Seek new understandings rather than remain in a rut because "that's the way it has always been done."

Seek help. Ask trusted friends for advice or assistance.

Have an accountability partner. Find someone to hold you accountable for the commitments and actions steps of your Plan.

Recruit a fellow participant. Find someone who is also interested in making changes in their life and travel the path together. Not only can they support you, but you can help them succeed. Your paths do not need to be the same: the purpose is encouragement, not counsel.

Maximize use of your strengths. If you are making significant changes in your life, utilize your strengths to assist in your success. You are likely to be more successful if you use your existing strengths than your weaknesses.

Make good decisions. Much of our success in life occurs when we make right, good, and proper choices. If this has been difficult for you in the past, make this one of your action steps. If you need a quick review, read the Appendix titled, "Wise Decision-Making" at the end of this book.

Apply filters. Filter out of your life people, places, and situations that create temptations that would hinder your goal to achieve the Integrity Life Principle. For example, if you are fighting an alcohol addiction, you should not spend time in bars. If you are having trouble with honesty and integrity, you can't associate with people who lie and are untrustworthy.

Review the "IMPLEMENTATION TECHNIQUES" above and determine which techniques might be effective for your purposes. Include those techniques as action steps on your initial list.

Step #3 – CHARACTER ISSUES

Look back over Chapters 10 and 11 and identify situations that will make your commitment to the Integrity Life Principle difficult to achieve. Also, think about actions that would make the Life Principle easier to achieve if they existed or were true. Then write out action steps that would advance your ability to achieve honesty, integrity, and truth in your life.

> 1. What personal characteristics in the "Life Analysis – Know Yourself" section need to be modified in order to achieve the Integrity Life Principle?
>
> 2. Think about the times or situations when you have not been honest, lived with integrity, or based your life on truth. Develop initial action steps that would prevent those situations from occurring or at least be under your control in the future.

Step #4 – LIFE VALUES

What Life Values (core values, priorities and commitments) require action steps in order to achieve the Integrity Life Principle? Add them to your list.

Step #5 – WHAT IF I FAIL

Do you need any action steps relative to what you will do if something fails? If you don't add an action step for this issue, think about the possible situations and know what you are going to do if they occur.

Step #6 – BRAIN STORMING

If you aren't satisfied with your list, try to think of other options. If you can't do that on your own, get a few friends to help you brainstorm the topics on which you need more input. The purpose here is to accumulate ideas, not evaluate them. You will do the evaluating later. Seek any kind of ideas! Often one seemingly crazy idea leads to a very good one.

Step #7 – CULL AND CONSOLIDATE

You should have a substantial list of steps and ideas after doing all of the above. Now it's time to finalize your initial list.

1. Reduce the list to the good and workable ideas. Remove anything you do not want to keep on your list.

2. Eliminate or combine the duplicates into similar groupings or headings.

3. Consolidate the similar ideas into one. You may want to have sub-points for the larger ideas.

4. Prioritize the groups. Within each group, prioritize the ideas.

5. Save this list permanently.

EXAMPLES

Your list might include statements like:

> a. I will be completely honest in all my business dealings. During the next year I will have my partner check all my proposals.
>
> b. I will be completely honest with my spouse. If I catch myself in a lie, I will admit it and correct it immediately.
>
> c. I will never make a promise dependent on someone else keeping their promise.
>
> d. I will not steal anything from my employer. If I do, I will return it immediately.
>
> e. I will take complete responsibility for my actions. I will admit mistakes and not shift blame.
>
> f. I will not take action based on what others say is true. I will independently confirm the truth.

LIFE PLANNING ADVICE

GENERAL

Depending on your circumstances, adopting integrity as a Life Principle could be challenging and require courage on your part. Don't give up if the road gets a bit bumpy. If honesty and truth have historically been a problem for you, it will take some time to build up trust with others who know about your failures. Be sincere and genuine and don't give up. Define good personal core values and intentionally commit to them in your life.

KEY TO SUCCESS

We believe that a key attribute for success is perseverance. Assuming you have a real desire to change, you must be patient. Make it a personal challenge that you will remain steadfast, no matter what happens. No matter what people may think or say, remain committed. The reward will be worth it.

FINAL ACTION STEPS

SUBJECT: **Honesty, Integrity, and Truth**

GOAL: **To be honest, live with integrity, and base my life on truth.**

FINAL ACTION STEPS:
Choose the 4 to 6 best action steps from your initial list and enter them below

1.

_____

_____

_____

2.

_____

_____

_____

3.

_____

_____

4.

_____

_____

5.

_____

_____

6.

_____

_____

_____

<u>TECHNOLOGY:</u> Consider entering information or reminders

on your phone, tablet, or computer.

REVIEW

Before you finalize your Action Steps, you should step back and take a broader look at what you have prepared.

1. CORE VALUES & PRIORITIES: Are your action steps consistent with your core values and revised life priorities?

_____

_____

2. FAMILY: Are your action steps consistent with your family's expectations?

_____

_____

  a. Do you need to tell any of your family members about your plans?
  b. Do you want to ask a family member for help?
  c. Will anything you do in this plan impact a family member? If so, you may need to talk with them before you start.

3. PERSONAL COMMITMENT: Are your action steps consistent with your personal desires and commitments? Are you ready to make these changes in your life? Are you missing anything important?

_____

Go back and modify your plans, if necessary.

GETTING STARTED

If you are excited and ready to begin, go for it! Begin with any or all of the above action steps.

But if you have any fear or reluctance, start slowly. There is absolutely no reason to try to do everything at once. Choose the action step that you think will be the easiest to achieve and get started. When that is implemented, choose the next easiest action step, and proceed through the list in that manner.

Some people may have a preference to do the most difficult one first and get that out of the way. That's fine if that works for you, but if this is going to create significant change in your life, we recommend you start slowly.

Chapter 14

Planning Part 5

Ongoing Progress Review and Evaluation

INTEGRITY LIFE PRINCIPLE:

Be honest, live with integrity, and base your life on truth.

"The life which is unexamined is not worth living."
Socrates[42]

FREQUENCY:

During the first eight weeks, review your plans weekly. In fact, as long as you have a significant list of action steps to accomplish you should take time weekly to evaluate your progress. At some point you can move to every two weeks and then monthly. As long as you still have things you want to implement, you should review your plan monthly.

We recommend you put this review time on your calendar and allow 90 minutes for your first review and update. Based on the time needed for your first review you can schedule future reviews.

SUCCESS:

Review your plan for success and failure. What can you discontinue, what should you add, and what have you achieved? Think particularly about your goals and priorities. How are you doing? Are you making progress?

MODIFICATION:

What can be removed because it has been successfully implemented? What is not working? What needs to be changed? What other action steps or ideas did you set aside when you developed your initial list? Should any of these ideas be added you your plan?

Make the necessary changes and tell a friend about your successes!

Check List

If you like to use check lists in completing tasks we have included a check list in Appendix C that lists all the steps in completing your Plan.

Chapter 15

Hope
&
Encouragement

*What you place your hope in
will define the path for your life.*

General

In "*Animal Dreams*" Barbara Kingsolver writes, *"The very least you can do in your life is figure out what you hope for. And the most you can do is live inside that hope. Not admire it from a distance but live right in it, under its roof."*[66]

Hope is a very important component of our existence. You may not always be conscious of your hope, but it's what drives you forward; it is the inherent desire of your heart. It is often masked by other mental or emotional baggage, but it is there nevertheless.

Kingsolver's point is that we need to unmask that hope, embrace it, and intentionally bring it into our lives. We must not just think about it or admire it, but make it a part of our lives. Why? Because what we hope for will define the course of our lives. It defines what is ultimately important to us and it will shape our priorities.

What do you hope for?

MERRIAM-WEBSTER's definition of hope is to desire, with the expectation of obtaining the object of that desire. Genuine hope is not wishful thinking, but a firm assurance about things that are "unseen" and still in the future.

Hope looks ahead to a future expectation that is uplifting or optimistic. The opposite of hope is depression, sadness, or dejection. We can have different hopes for the many parts of our lives. Some are little hopes and others are large. Some may be huge. Lives can be built and lost on the nature of our hope.

What are your hopes? Take a few minutes before you proceed to think about and identify some of your hopes. What do you hope for? What hope sustains you? Are you conscious of your hopes? What hope would sustain you if you were living in dire circumstances? Jot down some notes about your thoughts on "hope:"

_____

_____

_____

_____

_____

_____

_____

_____

_____

"Loyalty is what makes us trust.
Trust is what makes us stay.
Staying is what makes us love,
and love is what gives us hope."
Glenn van Dekken[67]

The Result of Hope

Many wise sayings about hope indicate that righteous people hope for joy or happiness but the destiny of wicked people is misery. What does it mean that the righteous hope for joy? Why joy? What is joy? Someone with joy has an inner peace, they are at rest, and they have a feeling of well-being. Typically joyful people are confident, assured, and have frequent feelings of happiness. If you ask them what or how they are feeling, they will often respond, *"Great!"*

Hope placed in evil and wickedness will not end well. Trouble is on the horizon, if it has not already arrived. Problems, and suffering are the typical results for making bad choices, usually the result of bad information, bad advice, or poor thinking.

Such trouble and suffering means loss, depression, mental anguish, lack of energy, and general despair. People often describe this feeling as "heartache." It can be said that this produces a broken spirit which can be debilitating because one feels lost, that no one cares, and life does not seem worthwhile. The meaning of life has been lost.

What meaning does life have for you?

"They say a person needs just three things
to be truly happy in this world:
someone to love, something to do,
and something to hope for."
Tom Bodett[68]

Three Psychiatrists

In the period leading up to WW2 there were three Jewish psychiatrists: two learned masters in the field, and one young apprentice. The first master was a man named Sigmund Freud. He had spent years studying people, striving to understand what made people tick. He had reached the conclusion that the most basic drive in the human being was the drive for pleasure. He concluded that it is our need for pleasure that explains why we do what we do, how we live.

The second master was Alfred Adler. He too spent years studying human behavior. His studies led him to disagree with Sigmund Freud. Adler was convinced that the explanation for human behavior was power. All of us grow up feeling inferior and powerless. He concluded that life was a drive to gain control, to feel we are important.

The third man was a young up-and-coming psychiatrist by the name of Victor Frankl. He hoped to follow in the footsteps of his mentors. But before his career gained any momentum WW2 started. The Nazis invaded and life became dangerous for Jews. Freud and Adler were world renowned scholars and managed to escape before Hitler invaded. Frankl was not so lucky. He was arrested and thrown into a Nazi concentration camp for four long years.

After the war was over, Frankl was released from the concentration camp and resumed his career. As he reflected upon his time as a prisoner, he realized something quite strange: the people who survived were not always the ones you'd expect. Many who were physically strong wasted away and died. Others who were seemingly physically weak survived. Why? What was it that enabled them to hang on through a living hell?

Frankl reflected on the theories of his mentors. Freud's pleasure principle couldn't explain it. For desperate and terrible years the people in that camp knew only pain, suffering and degradation. Pleasure was not a word in their vocabulary. It wasn't pleasure that kept them going.

What then of Adler's theory about power being the basic human need? That didn't hold up well either. Frankl and his fellow Jews were completely powerless during their time in the concentration camps. Each day they stared down the barrels of loaded guns, were treated like animals, and suffered jackboots on their faces. They had no power and no prospect of power.

Victor Frankl came up with his own theory. The difference between those who survived and those who perished was *hope*. Those who survived never gave up their belief that their lives had meaning, that despite everything going on around them, this period would one day end and they would again live meaningful and purposeful lives.[69]

The one thing that gives life value, that gives us purpose, is that we live with a sense of hope and that our life has meaning. If there is no meaning in life, then why bother? Life reverts to chaos where there is no purpose and hope – no meaning. Do I exist to give myself pleasure and then disappear into the mist without meaning? Does that make any sense to you? There are people who believe that nonsense. I don't. I firmly believe that I exist because life does have meaning.

> *"Once you choose hope,*
> *anything's possible."*
> Christopher Reeve[70]

The Time is Now

Life goes by quickly. Elderly people looking back at their youth are particularly and poignantly aware of the passing years. The prime of life is fleeting. Thus, it is wise not to put off until tomorrow what you can do today. The time is *now*. If you do it now you won't forget about it, and won't have to worry about getting it done before some deadline. You may even be able to enjoy the fruit of your labor.

This is good advice for everyone, but particularly important for those in the prime of life. We certainly have enough freedom in life to do most of the things we want and we should and can enjoy life. Although we are often told to follow our hearts, we also need to use wisdom in making good choices.

What is Your Hope?

List the most significant "hopes" in your life? Quiet your spirit and take time to really think about what you truly hope for. What are your life hopes? What are the deep desires of your heart?

_____

_____

_____

_____

_____

_____

_____

_____

_____

_____

Following are some possibilities:

1. that I am right with my God.
2. that I am a faithful and loving spouse or parent.
3. that I am a faithful and true leader in my family.
4. that I am a valued friend.
5. that my children have genuine joy in life.
6. that I use my skills, gifts, and resources wisely.
7. that I am honest and true, never misleading anyone.
8. that I serve my community well.
9. that my children marry spouses who truly love them.
10. that I impact and improve someone's life.
11. that I have a life of good health.
12. that my extended family truly love one another.
13. that I will marry the love of my life.
14. that I will live to spoil my grandbabies.
15. that I will live to see my grandchildren marry.

Now go back to <u>your</u> list and identify the top five and prioritize them. How do your hopes fit with your Life Plan? Are they in harmony with your plans?

> *"Hope itself is like a star – not to be seen*
> *in the sunshine of prosperity, and only*
> *to be discovered in the night of adversity."*
> Charles H. Spurgeon[71]

Don't Hope in Wealth

If one or more of your hopes is in money or wealth, erase it, or cross it out. Destroy it! Hope placed in wealth fails. It is fleeting. It is fickle and it will not last. Hope in wealth comes from worldly values that disappear and can be lost forever at any time. The problem is we can tend to fall in love with money and the power it brings. Loving luxury, power, and wealth is at the root of so much trouble.

The Source of Hope

Many proverbs and wise sayings identify the source of hope as "wisdom." Wisdom is permanent. It is extremely valuable because it can guide your decisions in life. Wisdom can give us a future so we have something to look forward to (to hope in). It will not fade away like a mist after a storm. It will not vanish in the face of trouble.

Wisdom will guide us in making right decisions.

ATTITUDES AND ACTIONS THAT ENCOURAGE HOPE

- Be patient!
- Share your difficulties with a trusted friend.
- Don't be constantly critical of life.
- Focus on what's important. Give little time to the little things.
- Understand that life has challenges. Everyone experiences tough times. You are not alone in that.
- Don't live in fear. Learn and grow from difficult times. Seek understanding from life situations.
- Be kind to yourself. Celebrate victories.
- Life is a journey, not a party.
- Be content with what you have.
- Be intentional: choose hope instead of fear.

TIPS FOR BEING HOPEFUL:

- Look on the bright side. Be an optimist, not a pessimist. Be positive and encourage others.
- Have an attitude of gratitude. Be a thankful person.
- See the humor in the human condition. Laugh at yourself. Don't take life too seriously.
- Listen to <u>good</u> music, read <u>good</u> books, watch <u>good</u> movies, and have <u>good</u> friends . . . (GIGO).
- Be healthy: take care of yourself physically (sleep, food, drink, and exercise).
- Avoid bad habits: alcohol, drugs, immorality, etc.
- Live and work in positive surroundings. Minimize exposure to negative influences.
- Have a life plan. Set goals. Know where you are going. Have a sense of purpose.
- Be organized. Have a to-do list and a schedule.

"Hope is medicine for a soul that's sick and tired."

Eric Swensson[72]

Chapter 16

Implementation Techniques

<u>Self-Discipline</u>

Self-discipline is a necessary character trait for implementing significant change in your life. Change requires an orientation toward living life in a certain manner and needs a systematic approach to problems, opportunities, or challenges.

Self-discipline is a basic life skill which is needed to achieve any significant life goal. In this Series we also use the term "intentionality" to represent this skill. It is extremely difficult to achieve any form of life improvement without discipline and intentionality.

IMPORTANCE OF SELF-DISCIPLINE

1. Focus.
Self-discipline helps you to stay focused on your goals. When we are not focused, other life activities can interfere with our intentions.

2. Respect.
Self-discipline will earn the respect of others. Even those who don't practice self-discipline will admire it in others. It is easy to become a role model if you practice self-discipline.

3. Self-confidence.
Self-discipline helps one accomplish tasks and overcome problems, therefore, it produces self-confidence.

4. Self-control.
An undisciplined person often lacks self-control. It is much easier to give in to temptations when self-control is not present. Those without self-control will often find themselves violating their core values.

5. Education and learning
Education requires self-discipline in study and preparation. Listening is an important personal trait.

6. Stress.
Being self-disciplined will enable you to get work done on time, which is often not the case if you procrastinate. The result of completing work in a timely manner will reduce stress and bring a level of contentment that makes life easier.

Intentionality

A good life, success, and happiness don't just happen. You cannot fix the results of bad choices simply by being sorry you made them. A better life starts with making good decisions, making commitments, and fixing mistakes. Being intentional!

The easy part here is making the decision to do something. The harder part is carrying out the decisions you make. The real test comes when those decisions result in problems. Are you going to turn tail and run at the first sight of trouble? Be prepared for difficulties and realize that the only answer is to persevere. Be self-disciplined.

Tips for Being Self-disciplined

AUTOPILOT:
What percentage of your life is on autopilot? Are your actions, responses, and activities being done without much thought and very little, if any, passion? You must get your life off autopilot.

GOALS:
You need to know what you want out of life. Be intentional about getting it. Have you established life goals that are guiding

your daily routines? Do you have core values that guide your life decisions?

TAKE CHARGE

1. Adopt the motto, "I can do this."

2. Accept and take responsibility for your decisions. If you make a mistake, correct it and move on.

3. Reject the concept that, "This is just the way things are."

4. Adopt actions that will enhance your chance for success:

    a. Control your calendar. Don't be too busy to succeed!

    b. Have a plan and work it.

    c. Be positive. Abandon all negative self-talk.

    d. Simplify your life, if necessary.

5. Be focused. Make your yes a YES, and your no a NO.

6. Be in control of your life. Make timely decisions. Don't allow life to simply happen to you.

BUILDING BLOCKS

1. Acquire knowledge in order to generate understanding that will ultimately produce wisdom.
2. Recognize that every decision has a consequence.
3. Decide what you are going to do. Commit to persevering.
4. Know the landscape! What is impacting your life today? What is working or not working? What should change?
5. Are you fearful? What are those fears? Are the fears valid? Address the fears you have.
6. Use your strengths and weaknesses? Build on your strengths and minimize reliance on your weaknesses.

If you are not intentional – nothing happens!

Applying Filters
FOUR KEY DECISIONS

How are you going to harness your heart and mind to produce the results you desire? What are the steps you can take to control what you see? How do you establish limits on what you hear? What should you avoid?

Important steps to begin: First, you must want to make improvements in your life. Second, you must intentionally take action that will either limit your exposure to negative input or open up new possibilities. Third, just get started. Take one step at a time.

Major Decision #1: I will filter what I see.

What are you reading? What are you watching on TV, the Internet, or your phone? What are you seeing that is causing or creating difficulty in the area of your life you are examining? If your problem is the TV, turn it off. If you can't do that, cancel the service. News is no longer news. News has become a channel to control your way of thinking. Be aware of the real influence of what you are watching or reading.

Decision #2: I will filter what I hear.

What are you hearing that could be causing difficulties for you? I realized some time ago it wasn't good for my mental health to listen to talking heads argue. I also realized I couldn't trust the truthfulness of what was being said. So, I just stopped! Choose what you hear with forethought. The music we listen to will often influence us more than we think. Reject the singers attempt to influence or poison your mind.

Decision #3: I will filter where I go.

Where are you going that is contributing to your difficulties? Avoid places that create negative temptations. If I am an alcoholic, I should not go to bars. If I have a gambling problem, I should not go to casinos or visit online gambling sites. The challenge is in choosing to cross or not to cross the line. You simply must make the decision ahead of time to avoid places that feed your weakness.

Decision 4: I will filter what I say.

Is your mouth causing you problems and getting you into trouble? Many of us are very careless about our speech and the impact it has on other people. The one who speaks too quickly or speaks without thinking can cause himself unnecessary difficulties.

Always bear in mind that words can have a gigantic negative impact. Therefore, you must carefully guard what you say. Words can start fires or put them out. Your goal should be gracious speech that is polite and shows respect.

Appendix A – How to Prioritize

General

What are your objectives? What's most important considering your responsibilities, plans, and goals? You will need to be relentless in sticking to your priorities. Remember your priorities change and evolve over time.

General questions to think about and guide the process of setting priorities:

- What needs to be done _now_?
- What is most important and bring the biggest gain?
- What happens if it doesn't get done?
- When do you need to begin?
- What materials, resources and skills do you need to accomplish the objective?

The Process

1. MAKE A LIST
Write a list of all your tasks. Identify any due dates for time-sensitive tasks. It is important to maintain an up-to-date list and also wise to keep an electronic back-up of the master list. Your master "to-do" list serves as a running log of what you want to accomplish over time.

2. ASSIGN STATUS / TIME FRAME
Assign an appropriate time frame. For example, this task needs to be accomplished today, this week, this month, this quarter, or this year. Where possible identify the date you want to begin.

3. URGENCY/IMPORTANCE/PRIORITY

Identify the urgent versus the important tasks. Ignore anything else unless your list is <u>very</u> short. Choose one of the following methods:

a. Scale Method: On a scale of 1 to 10 (or 1 to 100) assess value or importance.

b. Other Simple Strategies

- Do the most important task first.
- Do the most impactful task first.
- Complete one major important task before you move on to the next task.
- Do a simple high/medium/low assignment.

4. FLEXIBILITY

Be flexible. Situations and circumstances can change very quickly. Re-evaluate your priority list frequently. If priorities change move on to the next priority. Know when to stop working on a goal or action step. Make sure that what you are doing warrants your time.

Appendix B – Check List

If you like to use check lists in completing tasks, we have included a check list that lists all the steps in completing the Plan.

Chapter 10: Planning Part 1 – Life Analysis, Know Yourself

- ☐ List the things and activities you love to do.
- ☐ List your greatest physical or mental skills and abilities.
- ☐ List your strengths, special skills, and serious passions.
- ☐ List your weaknesses.
- ☐ List any roadblocks, distractions, or hindrances that might prevent you from implementing the Integrity Life Principle.
- ☐ List any serious character flaws.

Chapter 11: Planning Part 2 – Life Values

- ☐ List your final 5 to 8 Core Values.
- ☐ List your top 6 to 12 Life Priorities today.
- ☐ How would your Life Priorities change if you knew you had only two years to live?
- ☐ How would the Integrity Life Principle or any new objectives change your current Life Priorities?
- ☐ How should the Life Analysis in Chapter 10 change your Priorities?
- ☐ Given the Integrity Life Principle, what new priorities would you need to adopt?
- ☐ Prepare a final list of your revised Life Priorities. Aim at 6 to 8, but no more than 12.
- ☐ List the existing traits, behaviors, activities, or habits you must manage in order to achieve the Integrity Life Principle.
- ☐ List your final 4 to 8 Life Commitments.

Chapter 12: Planning Part 3 – Integrity Life Principle

The Life Goal is: *I will be honest, live with integrity, and base my life on truth.*

Chapter 13: Planning Part 4 – Action Steps

☐ Select and list of the best 4 to 10 tips. The tips are located on pages 27, 47, 53, 61, 75.

☐ Choose the top 4 to 6 tips and list them in priority order.

☐ Choose and list the implementation techniques that would be helpful to you in implementing your plan.

☐ Produce and list your initial list of actions steps for making the Integrity Life Principle a reality in your life.

☐ Cull and consolidate the initial list.

☐ List action steps for those situations that will make your commitment to the Integrity Life Principle difficult to achieve.

☐ List the existing personal characteristics that must be improved to achieve your objectives.

☐ List the core values, priorities, or commitments that require action steps in order to achieve the Integrity Life Principle.

☐ List the 2 to 6 "Tips For Improvement" that you feel would be particularly effective for you.

☐ Reduce the working list to only the good and workable ideas. Eliminate or combine the duplicates.

☐ Identify and list the helpful "TECHNIQUES FOR IMPLEMENTATION" that warrant inclusion in your action steps.

☐ List action steps relative to what you will do if something fails.

☐ Cull and consolidate the list.

☐ Prioritize the groups and the individual actions within groups.

☐ FINAL ACTION STEPS: Choose the 4 to 6 best action steps from your list.

☐ TECHNOLOGY: Consider entering information or reminders on your phone, tablet, or computer.

☐ REVIEW:

   a) Are your action steps consistent with your core values and revised life priorities?

   b) Are your action steps consistent with your family's expectations? Do you need to communicate with your family?

   c) Are your action steps consistent with your personal desires and commitments?

☐ Modify your plans as necessary.

Chapter 14: Planning Part 5 – Ongoing Progress Review

☐ During the first eight weeks, review your plans weekly.

☐ Review your plan for success and failure. Make necessary changes.

☐ Modify and update your plan as needed.

Transformation Roadmap
Wisdom That Transforms!

1. Honesty builds trust and reduces stress. Living an honest life fosters trust, admiration, and reliability in relationships, while also reducing the stress and anxiety that come from maintaining lies or fearing exposure.

2. Lies can destroy reputations, relationships, and opportunities, often leading to shame, isolation, or worse. Admitting mistakes and taking responsibility for wrongdoing is the only path to redemption and personal growth.

3. Integrity is not about appearances or reputation it is about living truthfully and morally, even when no one is watching. It provides a foundation for respect and trust from others.

4. Integrity shields you from chaos and consequences. Being honest protects you from the stress, guilt, and damaging consequences of the lack of trust. It fosters secure relationships, builds a positive reputation, and ensures a life of contentment and stability.

5. Never compromise your core values or integrity. Compromising on fundamental beliefs, ethical standards, or moral principles will lead to a loss of character and self-respect. Staying true to your values ensures a life of authenticity and inner peace.

6. Healthy compromise can foster cooperation and growth. In negotiations or relationships, compromise based on mutual respect and trust can create win-win outcomes. However, it should never come at the expense of your integrity or other core values.

7. Adhering to absolute truths, which transcend personal opinions or societal trends, anchors your life in timeless principles that guide ethical decisions and foster good character.

8. Truth is not subjective or changeable. A life built on integrity will avoid the moral confusion and societal disorder that arises when individuals have their own versions of the truth.

9. Truth is the foundation of character and integrity. Living truthfully and honestly in all aspects of life builds trust, reliability, and moral authority, ensuring your character remains untainted by deception or dishonesty.

10. Never compromise core values. It is essential to remain steadfast in upholding your core values and ethical standards, as compromising them can lead to a loss of honor and respect.

11. Core values and hope should be foundational in your life, shaping your priorities and defining your path.
Maintain a sense of hope and belief that your life has meaning, as this provides value and direction, helping you persevere through challenges.

12. Make informed decisions that align with your values. Thoughtful decision-making involves gathering information, considering consequences, and making choices that are in line with your ethical and spiritual standards.

Your decisions shape your life.
Start building with intention!

Free PDF
MAKE WISE DECISIONS

[Get the ebook version for 99 cents]

Consequences Shape Lives.

This book discusses the nature of decisions and explores eight essential questions to make better decisions.

You are a few decisions away from transforming your life. You can make better decisions! This resource has sections on what makes a poor decision, questions to ask yourself, traps to avoid, short and sweet decisions, the wise decision framework, and twenty ways to be wise. It also has a handy decision-making checklist. (12 pages)

Free PDF: https://getwisdompublishing.com/resource-registration/

Kindle ebook for 99 cents: https://www.amazon.com/dp/B0FG8NC53J

Ebook

Free PDF

Ten Steps to Wise Choices

Timeless Wisdom. Practical Tools. Lasting Impact.

Free PDF
Life Improvement Principles
[Get the ebook version for 99 cents]

You can live your best life!

Welcome to a journey of discovery! In case you have forgotten, your actions have consequences. Unlock your potential! This book (60+ pages) provides the overview of all our strategies and wisdom principles to live your best life. You *can* transform your life! Get your wisdom-based roadmap to a better life and unlock all the possibilities for growth and success.

Free PDF: https://getwisdompublishing.com/resource-registration/

Kindle ebook for 99 cents:
https://www.amazon.com/dp/B0FG883KZM

Ebook

Life Improvement Principles

You can live your best life!

Stephen H Berkey
J. S. Wellman

Free PDF

Make it your life goal to be the best you can be!

Discover Wisdom and live the life you deserve.

Your Next Steps
Change Your Life with purpose and intention!

Should you read other books in this series?

We recommend that if you acquire any books in the Series, you should also obtain *CHOOSE Integrity*. This is the foundational book in the series. We also believe the four books covering the other Primary Life Principles would be particularly useful for living a better life: Friends, Speech, Diligence (Work), and Money.

CHOOSE Faith

This is a unique book in the Series. It addresses all the important spiritual type questions you might consider. It answers questions like: Does God exist? Why should I care about faith? What's religion all about? Does eternal life really exist? I don't know the right questions to ask. What is the truth? This book will help you find answers to your spiritual questions.

LIFE PLANNING HANDBOOK

This book is also unique. If you are interested in doing a complete life plan that covers all aspects of your life, not just a specific topic like those addressed in The Life Planning Series, go to:

https://www.amazon.com/dp/1952359325

You can live a better life.
Just Decide You Want to!

The Life Planning Series

These books can improve your life.

LIFE PLANNING HANDBOOK	**A Life Plan will shape your life journey!** The next step in your life planning.
CHOOSE INTEGRITY	**Life Principle:** Be honest, live with integrity, and base your life on truth.
CHOOSE FRIENDS WISELY	**Life Principle:** Choose your friends wisely.
CHOOSE THE RIGHT WORDS	**Life Principle:** Guard your speech.
CHOOSE GOOD WORK HABITS	**Life Principle:** Be diligent and a hard worker.
CHOOSE FINANCIAL RESPONSIBILITY	**Life Principle:** Make sound financial choices.

CHOOSE A POSITIVE SELF-IMAGE	**Life Principle:** Be confident in who you are.
CHOOSE LEADERSHIP	**Life Principle:** Lead well and be a loyal follower.
CHOOSE CORE VALUES	**Life Principle:** Core values will drive your life.
CHOOSE LOVE AND FAMILY	**Life Principle:** Build strong relationships.
CHOOSE FAITH	*Your Spiritual Guidebook for Questions about Religion, God, Heaven, Truth, Evil, and the Afterlife.*

Go to: **https://www.amazon.com/dp/B09TH9SYC4**

to get your copy.

Create a life based on purpose, meaning, and lasting fulfillment.

Acknowledgments

My wife has patiently persevered while I indulged my interest in this subject. Thank you for your patience.

Our older daughter has been an invaluable resource. She has also graciously produced our website at www.lifeplanningtools.com

Our middle daughter designed all the covers for this series. We are very grateful for her help, talent and creativity.

Notes

QUOTES

ACCURACY: We have used a number of quotes throughout this book that came from our files, notes, books, public articles, the Internet, etc. We have made no attempt to verify that these quotes were actually written or spoken by the person they are attributed to. Regardless of the source of these quotes, the wisdom of the underlying message is relative to the content in this book and worth noting, even if the source reference is erroneous.

SOURCE: Unless otherwise specifically noted below the quotes used herein can be sourced from a number of different websites on the Internet that provide lists of quotes by subject or author. The same or similar quotes will appear on multiple sites. Therefore, rather than assign individual quote sources, we are providing a list of sites where we might have found the quotes that were used in this book:

--azquotes.com
--codeofliving.com
--goodhousekeeping.com
--graciousquotes.com
--keepinspiring.me
--parade.com
--quotemaster.org
--success.com
--thoughtcatalog.com
--wisesayings.com

--brainyquote.com
--everydaypower.com
--goodreads.com/quotes
--inc.com
--notable-quotes.com
--plantetofsuccess.com
--quotir.com
--thoughtco.com
--wisdomquotes.com
--wow4u.com

1 Les Brown, see QUOTES above.
2 Stephen H Berkey, www.amazon.com/author/stephenhberkey
3 Latin American saying, see QUOTES above.
4 Aesop, see QUOTES above.
5 SermonCentral.com; contributed by Perry Greene.
6 --
7 --
8 A large number of Internet sites. Search for "Jonathan Edwards," "Max Jukes," or "A. E. Winship."
9 Roger Crawford, see QUOTES above.
10 Cicero, see QUOTES above.
11 Jimi Hendrix, see QUOTES above.
12 Henri Frederic Amiel, see QUOTES above.
13 Survey Findings: tp://www.creditdonkey.com/lying.html.
14 *Culture Clips*, Plugged In, June 2006, p. 2.
15 *How Honest Are You?* Reader's Digest, Jan 2004.
16 Abe Lincoln, see QUOTES above.
17 Billy Graham, see QUOTES above.
18 Richelle E. Goodrich, see QUOTES above.

19 Immanuel Kant, see QUOTES above.

20 Oprah Winfrey, see QUOTES above.

21 John Maxwell, see QUOTES above.

22 Thomas S. Monson, see QUOTES above.

23 Mahatma Gandhi, see QUOTES above.

24 Ludwig Erhard, see QUOTES above.

25 Unknown, see QUOTES above.

26 Dennis Prager, see QUOTES above.

27 Mahatma Gandhi, see QUOTES above.

28 Bible, Book of Philippians, 1:27—4:1.

29 Alan K. Simpson, see QUOTES above.

30 Andy Rooney, see QUOTES above.

31 Josh McDowell, *Evidence That Demands A Verdict*, Thomas Nelson publisher, ISBN: 9781401676704.

32 --

33 Jodi Picoult, see QUOTES above.

34 Alexander Solzhenitsyn, Ray Blunt, "Courage in the Corridors," http://govleaders.org/courage.htm

35 Abraham Lincoln, see QUOTES above.

36 Amy Morin, LCSW [Medically reviewed by Ann-Louise T. Lockhart, ABPP, *Steps to Stop a Child From Lying*, https://www.verywellfamily.com/steps-help-child-stop-lying-tell-the-truth-1094945, August 31, 2020,

37 Marvin Williams, see QUOTES above.

38 Thomas S. Monson, see QUOTES above.

39 Kenneth Blanchard, see QUOTES above.

40 Les Brown, see QUOTES above.

41 Brian Tracy, see QUOTES above.

42 Socrates, see QUOTES above.

43 Amelia Earhart, see QUOTES above.

44-65 *-none-*

66 Barbara Kingsolver. *Animal Dreams*, Harper Perennial; Reissue edition (2013), ISBN-13: 978-0062278500.

67 Glenn van Dekken, see QUOTES above.

68 Tom Bodett, see QUOTES above.

69 Victor Frankl, Based on a talk given by Australian speaker Michael Frost.

70 Christopher Reeve, see QUOTES above.

71 Charles H. Spurgeon, see QUOTES above.

72 Eric Swensson, see QUOTES above.

About the Author

The author graduated from the Business School at Indiana University and obtained a master's degree at Georgia State University in Atlanta. His first career was as a senior executive with a top insurance and financial institution, where he spent a number of years directing strategic planning for one of their major divisions.

In the 1990s he founded an online Internet business which he sold in 2010. He began to write and publish books and materials that led to an interest in personal life planning. This resulted in combining the wisdom of wise sayings and proverbs with life planning and the result is the Life Planning Series and the Life Planning Handbook.

The author, his wife, and two of his children and their families live in the Nashville, TN area.

WEBSITE: http://www.lifeplanningtools.com

AMAZON: www.amazon.com/author/jswellman

Contact Us

	www.lifeplanningtools.com info@lifeplanningtools.com	Website Email
Facebook	JSWellman	
	www.amazon.com/author/jswellman	**Author Page**
Life Planning Series	www.amazon.com/dp/B09TH9SYC4	
	www.lifeplanningtools.link/newsletter	**Monthly News Letter**

You can help

IDEAS and SUGGESTIONS: If you have a suggestion to improve this book, please let us know.

Mention our LIFE PLANNING books on your social platforms and recommend them to your family and friends.

Thank you!

Make a Difference

*"The law of prosperity is generosity.
If you want more, give more."*
Bob Proctor[57]

Have you ever done something just out of kindness or goodwill without wanting or expecting anything in return? I'm going to ask you to do <u>two things</u> just for that reason. The first will be just out of the goodness of your heart and the second to make an impact in someone else's life.

It won't cost you anything and it won't take a lot of time or effort.

This Book

First, what did you think of this book? Give the book an honest review in order for us to compete with the giant publishers. What did you like and how did it impact you? It will only take you several minutes to leave your review at: https://www.amazon.com/dp/1952359309

Follow the link above to the Amazon sales page, scroll down about three quarters of the page and click the box that says: "Write a customer review." It does not have to be long or well-written — just tell other readers what you think about the book. Or, just score the book on a scale of 1 – 5 stars (5 is high).

This will help us a great deal and we so appreciate your willingness to help. If you want to tell us something about the book directly, you can email us at: info@lifeplanningtools.com.

Give Books to Students and Employees

Secondly, do you know any schools or organizations that might want to give this book or our Life Planning Handbook to their students or employees?

Here is how you can help. If you send us the contact information and allow us to use your name, we will contact the person or persons you suggest with all the details. Obviously there would be special pricing and if the order is large enough, a message from the organization's CEO could be included on the printed pages.

Alternatively, you can personally give a copy of one of our books to the organization for their consideration. We would recommend our Life Planning Handbook, but some organizations might be interested in a specific subject. If they are interested in this partnership with us, they should contact us directly.

It is not that difficult to help someone live a better life: just a little time and intentionality. Let us hear from you if you want to make a difference in someone's life!

J. S. Wellman
Extra-mile Publishing
steve@lifeplanningtools.com
www.lifeplanningtools.com

Wisdom Without Action is Just information!

INTEGRITY LIFE PRINCIPLE: Be honest, live with integrity, and base your life on truth.

LIFE PLANNING SERIES
J.S. WELLMAN

INTEGRITY LIFE PRINCIPLE: Be honest, live with integrity, and base your life on truth.

LIFE PLANNING SERIES
J.S. WELLMAN

www.ingramcontent.com/pod-product-compliance
Lightning Source LLC
Chambersburg PA
CBHW060322050426
42449CB00011B/2607